MW00677936

BEST POETS OF 2019

VOL. 4

John T. Eber Sr.
MANAGING EDITOR

A publication of

Eber & Wein Publishing

Pennsylvania

Best Poets 2019: Vol. 4
Copyright © 2020 by Eber & Wein Publishing as a compilation.

Library of Congress
Cataloging in Publication Data

ISBN 978-1-60880-666-9

Proudly manufactured in the United States of America by

Eber & Wein Publishing
Pennsylvania

A note from the editor

"We are half-survivors
Cast up upon these shores"
from "Refuge" (page 1)

When we began accepting poems for this series last September, little did any of us know the crisis we would find ourselves amidst come March 2020. When ninety-eight-year-old Irene Backalenick, once a writer for the *New York Times*, wrote her poem "Refuge" last year, little did she know that her sentiments *then* would take on a prophecy of their own when *now*, less than a year later, nursing homes and assisted living facilities across the nation would account for the majority of sicknesses and deaths throughout a nationwide (and global) pandemic. Little did she know that hospitals in every state would become "wreckage" sites for thousands of "half-survivors" and those not even that lucky.

In 2019, the care and compassion given by first responders, nurses, and medical staff had a profound impact on Irene's life as well as many lives of those sequestered in nursing homes. Today, the dedication and selflessness exuding from this group is having a profound impact on the world and on the lives of patients of all ages. The "brittle," depleted, hopeless scene Irene eloquently illustrates through metaphor has become a static scene on the news every day of the week. For now beaches will remain closed and "lifeless," but one thing is certain: like Irene and her fellow half-survivors, we will emerge from this crisis a "new-formed world" and all because of the refuge lovingly and unceasingly provided by medical professionals from coast to coast.

I hope for many this volume offers a brief reprieve from the monotony of quarantine life. The mind, however, can never be contained; therefore, keep it nourished by continuing to write.

Be well,
John Eber Sr.

Refuge

We are half-survivors
Cast up upon these shores
Twisted shards of wreckage
Maimed and broken, addled, dazed
Like brittle wall-eyed fish
Abandoned here at low tide
Or half-empty lifeless shells
No longer mollusk homes

But, wait, in this ungiving scene
Arise the first responders
These nurses, aides, and staffers
Building new sand castles
With certainty, compassion
With soft and caring hands
Dedicated, educated, goal-driven
Daily thus a new-formed world
And this unlikely wreckage
Turns once again to life

Irene Margolis Backalenick
Bridgeport, CT

I was a working journalist for years, writing for The New York Times and other national publications. In my sixties, I acquired a PhD in theater history and turned to theater criticism, a career I then pursued for some thirty years. When I moved to this senior facility in my nineties, I found a new genre—poetry. My poem "Refuge," written recently at age ninety-eight, was inspired by Watermark, the facility where I live.

2019: This World Is Changing

This world is changing, and everything in it
Most humans and beasts are able to see it

Cold, droughts, fires, floods, and migration
Winds and wars
Many, many, many times raging
Because, this world is changing

Infectious diseases and bacteria emerge from common and far away places
Yes indeed, this world is changing

Crime, disparity, gridlock and violence in our societies
Are also changing
What was once unimaginable is now common
In all of our spaces and even in our holiest of places

This world is changing
Here, near, there, everywhere
Including far, far away places

So tell me my brother, my sister
Are you also able see what I see
Or is it just me
This world is changing

What will we do?
To fix this and make it anew
Because: This World is Changing

Guadalupe B. Rodriguez
Edinburg, TX

Broken

Being broken leaves most of us feeling, forever guilty and ashamed
Because we know that something is wrong, but we don't know who is to blame
So we just keep right on fighting, the fights we can and cannot win
And when the fight is over, we just begin to fight again
We fight the ones who love us, we fight people we don't even know
Because the one thing about being broken, is it leaves you with only one direction to go
And then one day along that path, you see something that you've never seen
A voice is calling out to you, and it says I love the broken things
So you take one step closer, but really there's two steps that are made
And you know that it was all worth it, when you feel that first embrace
And it's there that you find happiness, something you've always managed to elude
My darling it is my great honor, that I get to be broken with you

Shelby John Holley
Booneville, MS

The Graveyard

The old graveyard was on the south side of town and during Hallows eve night no one came around. The town's people told of eerie noises in the night and ghostly sightings behind the gates. The old graveyard had been around longer than the town, a resting place for crooks, thieves, cowpokes, bar flies, and thug's....until... respectability changed the graveyards residents to a... more.... (harrumph!)... respectable... clientele.

The north side of the graveyard now had mausoleums and gravestones made of marble and granite with angles and love sonnets engraved upon them. Gone were the wooden makers that announced how someone had died, hung with boots on or boots off, shot in the back or shot in the groin, and they were of the most unsavory kind.... and they resided right here on the cemetery grounds!

The town council decided to change the name "graveyard" to something more respectable and refined, and so "The Last Resting Place" is what the council decided upon. They would extend the section where the more affluent would reside and they reluctantly agreed to leave the dead where they lie on the south side of the cemetery yard.

All were agreed this was a suitable way to make death seem more respectable for the coming age....and, the township was growing, and new ideas were now in mode and respectability was needed in all aspects of the town's growth.

But, what of the old side, and what of the ghost that lived so happily there for ages and ages making the townspeople scared and what of the sightings and the ghostly appearance of fellows who had died and once again risen....on Hallows eve night?

Dianna Diaz
Tucson, AZ

Just a Story

she used to get up at the crack of dawn
he would sleep later

you were meant to be a farmer
he used to say and yes...

she would know and see in her mind's eye
the fields of hard work
her body and heart would thrive upon

she would see big open sky
flat lands all around and in the distance
the sun would shine so hard
making the tall golden grasses wave to her
caress her being invite...
singing her name in ethereal wind chime whispers
'wind speak' she would think, feel and know she was meant to be here

but...she wasn't there, only a dreamer she was

then one day her friend died
since that day she could not wake herself up

it was too much perhaps
the end of all losses, for she had endured many

now he rises with the dawn instead
she covers her head, closes her eyes...her ears
he bends down to kiss her goodbye

she waits till he's gone then cries

her greatest loss, she has forgotten how to dream
his greatest loss...the beautiful dreamer

Sharon Weimer
Aberdeen, NJ

Her

Her big beautiful eyes,
That once held the brightest of lights.
Were now dull and lifeless.
Her long, wavy hair,
Once had a shine that was everlasting.
But now,
It was volumeless.
She used to love the way
The light hit her mocha skin.
The way the wind used to caress her face,
Or even when the birds sang.
It happened in a blink of an eye,
Her once happy state became dark
And gloomy,
Dreamless even.
She was depressed,
But she kept everything together
With her biggest fake smile.
She slowly became void of any feelings,
Until she was nothing.

Shanja Marie Plains
Ferriday, LA

Still Hurt

Looking at the phone that never rings wondering why he hasn't called. Was he still mad from early? I call and call and still no answer. Am I scared out of my mind now? I put on my clothes and run to his house. As I am running to his house my play brother comes to me and says, "You haven't heard." I said, "Heard what?" "That Jamreiun is dead." I am thinking no no this can't be it's not true. "You're lying. He's not dead; I saw him earlier today. He's not dead." With tears in my eyes I race to his house. His house door wide open, his mom on the floor holding something to her chest crying real hard. I say "Is it true? Tell me it's not true. That's all I want to hear." She says it is. He is gone and he's not coming back. I started to cry. I fell to my knees saying no no no no. I go to his room and sit on his bed saying he's coming home, he's coming home. Hours I sat there and he didn't come through that door. I am crying my heart out saying I didn't get to say goodbye or I love you or I am sorry for all the things I said to you— forgive me please come back. I learned my lesson and I'll never do it again. We were supposed to grow old together. You were the one I needed and they took you from me. We had hope and dreams for the future. You were my rock now who am I without you? Who's going to love me like you? Who's going to stop my heart from being broken? I love you so much; I still do. I could never stop loving you. You were the one to make me smile and laugh. I miss you so much. If I had a day with you I would tell you I love you and miss you and am sorry and I need you to come back to me because I hate not seeing you. I miss talking to you. I need you here with me; there's so much stuff I want to tell you.
You are my world my heart my every thing. I know you want me to be strong but without you I am nothing. You're the only one who can make me change. I dream about you and I swear I saw you when I was outside but it wasn't. I cry all the time.

Shanell Norfleet
Chicago, IL

Summer Love

Maybe you're not healthy
Maybe that's not up to me
Maybe words are all a lie
Maybe love heals while we pretend to fly

Birds beat their wings every day
Muses come and go away
Like art, it colors your world
Then leaves fast in a dreadful twirl

They say they love me,
But what is love?
They say they want lifetime,
But I can only mutter - WHY?

Honesty is the fruit of my existence
And I wouldn't have it any other way
Slings and Arrows and Resistance
I'll speak from my heart and still smile even if you run away

But what if you stay...
What is it that I'm supposed to do if you stay?

I guess I'll keep on dancing
I hope you can keep up
Maybe we'll see a blessing
Promise I won't sleep; Gladly let thoughts of you keep me up
What sweet hugs
I'll think of you in the winter, my Sweet summer love

Sethea Seang
Los Angeles, CA

A Stubborn Soul

Cast down from the cosmos, she leaves behind
Father Sun and Mother Moon.
With her essence she brings emeralds, may flowers and high hopes,
magically flying in riding her loyal bull as she stubbornly copes.
She's fixed now;
she's firmly planted in Earth.
She's surviving, existing...
rooted in this shallow little valley while longing and dreaming
of what once was.

She's slowly slipping away, her innocent spirit fading fast.
Her heart is aching for a life of the past.

Yet, her strong soul lives on yearning,
Watching and waiting for that fateful moment
Mother Moon calls her home.

Amanda D. Gahm
Henryetta, OK

Lost Within Twilight

Wandering through the less traveled by road;
In the midst of the resurrecting morning mirth,
By the bewitching pine's forelock of green,
Pulsing the timeless beats of earth.

Haunting me with immortal pride,
By the lonely shores of an ocean of time,
Lies the overcast woods of solitary journeys,
A forsaken nightmare, with open eyes.

Through pathless forest of unfading thorns
Rises a mockingbird; thief of summer song,
Humming a wild tune beneath Night's nebulous sky,
Among the whispers of the ginkgo and the black willow's lies.

Perching amid the ghostly winds of the soul
Beyond the lavender of the midnight sea,
Fends a forgotten place along the stony way
Where desolate Night will always stay.

Sarah Flora Chocron
Wichita, KS

Nothing

My arms feel so weak and tired,
I don't want to move.
The body I control,
Has went out of control.
My mind has abandoned me,
I am a figment of my imagination.

My legs do not want to walk,
If I am not alone or full of sorrow.
The heart beats are gone.
I lay in my bed with my eyes wide open
I feel nothing

Nothing to think of as I stare at the ceiling
Nothing to move because all my limbs have stopped
Nothing to hold me from jumping off the first building I see
Nothing but one tear running down my face.
That tear is the key to the shelter that is my sanity

Sarah Wyley
Knoxville, TN

The Power of Love

Love is Beautiful
Love is Peace
Love is Life
Love is Light

Change is Hard
Change is Scary
Change is Tough
Change is Life

Heartbreak is Painful
Heartbreak is Hurtful
Heartbreak is Damaging
Heartbreak is Heartache

Love is Powerful
Love is Strength
Love is Uplifting
Love is Healing

Sarah Elizabeth Jones
LaGrange, IN

Angel

I met an angel
Disguised as a woman
The most beautiful of all things holy
She was not a regular angel
But a fallen one
I helped her repair her wings and she freed me of my sins
To me she speaks my religion
I will forever worship her undoubtedly

Revae Mitchell
Puyallup, WA

Shooting Star

I saw a shooting start tonight
I wished of someone
Someone to touch and to kiss
Someone to give me some sort of attention;
reassurance that I'm actually here
Someone to love me
I wished of someone calling me beautiful
I wished of someone filling this "void"
But when I realized something important
I saw a shooting start tonight
I wished for the love of myself
Because I need to learn self love before I can wish
for someone else to love me

Precious Ikia Goins
Glenmora, LA

I Found the Land of Fastasy

I will soon be leaving the land of fantasy.
I saw rainbows, little people, pirates, Indians, dragons and so much more.
Where immortality is living in harmony with Humanity
In totality
Right off shore.
I will soon be leaving the land of fantasy
Magic and mystery
Looking for an on core.
Where immortality is living in harmony with Humanity
I am looking for another novelty
To explore.
I will be leaving the land of fantasy
Which is now written in poetry
To be there forevermore
Where immortality is living in harmony with humanity
In versatility
To add to the lore.
I will soon be leaving the land of fantasy
Where immortality is living in harmony with Humanity.

Bette Anne Bavington
Brooksville, FL

Chaotic Minds

Trapped in their own chaotic mind
a writer is often misunderstood
Looked at as an object to admire
yet feared as a slave of insanity
Spilling their heart and soul onto
the paper laid out before them
Lost in a world of formative words
on display to all opened eyes
Closed minds scorn their mere existence
afraid to succumb to untold truths

Theresa Ann Belanger
Hoffman Estates, IL

A Prayer for My Mother

I said a prayer for you today.
It wasn't very long.
I asked the Lord to lift you up,
To guide, and keep you strong.
I asked Him to protect you,
And keep you safe from harm.
I asked the Lord to build your faith,
And hold you in His arms.
I asked the Lord,
"please bless my Mother!"
For like her, there's just no other!

Kathryn Elizabeth Pentland
Indianapolis, IN

My Country Siamese

I had a Siamese cat
She had a loud meow
She was so pretty
And sweet
Right down to her little brown feet.
My country Siamese
Would purr in her sleep
I sang her a song
That went like this....
I love you little darling
You make me so happy inside
Like rainbows in the skies
I love you pretty darling.
The town knew about you
And your walks in the day time
You always came back at night
To a simple knap and supper.
I loved you little darling
Like lovin your baby
Who is just a dumpling and all.
You made me happy all the time
As a star in the Texas sky
When the flowers were in bloom
My Siamese came out to play
In a field where birds flew away
She was my country cat all the way.

Sharon Ann Maloney
Hollywood, FL

Sleep Deprivation

I'm cold, and hot
I'm scared, and not
I'm high on something
Pretty sure I know, but it would be a low blow
Never knew I could rhyme like this
Gotta get my beautiful sleep bliss
I really should shut my eye
But then I would become deprived
Of the amazing things in store
As I flip through the non existing pages of lore
I now say my farewells
Just like all the well's
Good day, good night
Love days, love nights and all their creepy frights
Have a great shut eyes rest
And now maybe I should sleep, I think it's for the best
Goodbye one more
No more rhyming in store
Thy fair one is high indeed
And now she needs a steed
Feeding dogs and cats
Almost as hard as taming bats
Waking up in the wee hours of the morning to say hello
But only to get awoken to a heavy bellow
Ok though seriously thank you and good night
Have a blissful flight, I now soar away
High high above for the ending of today
On the sleepy train, to reach the sleeper plane

Piper Elisabeth Butts
Colorado Springs, CO

Saw Dust Woods

It is by the torture of my sin on my skin of the flesh. I never regret.
I detest more yes escape to rest at best sometimes.
When in this awake in mess the filth even discovered in deep regions of
the mind.
This is not a little conscience about ruin onto me.
Even for all that is done is not an accident reason or mistake feeding.
When I the sad it meant dread intent behind the murder of someone.
When past dead dark in the soul planted in some field or woods a body.
This is somehow light will show upon the dense area.
It is of a failure while tragic decomposed covenants the fifth alliance about
sores decode stagnant dreams.
It continues to the bleeding to defeating my health mentally marvelous.
This as beating obscure visions refers to situations involving intrigue.
Now to no understand fighting plans.
These were physically these an example sentences selected.
They have to had been transcended in vast discern common the concern
for humanity. It will be divided by money beliefs circumstances.
These are all the advances that it is towards technology.
Those are badly some force ignored extension cords the path of a paint in
planer forged.
It is to my discretion could connect without spark combustion.
A lesson destined for profit thought a top of list fit.
Is it in the sub conscience missed gap that absent? This would fall lines
magnetic from wrong doing once again The Systematic Cat
back under so doing those grew in testicles.

Reginald Brown
Houston, TX

Daffodils

Belittled by their words
I felt minuscule
Infinitesimal
In the immense world
Petrified
I was
Too scared to be me
They're words
Mimicked me
In a unkind tune
I was forced to swallow their monstrous words
Words that should be left unsaid
They forgot words speaks in an echo
An echo of death
Those words were the monsters under
My bed that haunted me at night
I couldn't escape the inevitable
I couldn't escape the reality of unreality
I couldn't be me
I cried myself to sleep wondering if there would be light to shine on me in
the obscure and clandestine world
But the daffodils
Their yellow petals , corolla and stigma made my heart warm with hope
The injustices those words committed should be thrown away then turned
to dust swept away and be forgotten
But they weren't
Everyday I was forced to swallow more and more until I couldn't chew
anymore
I couldn't breathe
I couldn't eat anymore
I didn't want to eat anymore
And they forgot the moral of a story

Shemar Jaheim Magee
Denver, CO

Let Go

It's okay to let go of the past,
For holding onto it won't bring it back.
You can let go of mistakes as well,
 For it's not a shame to sometimes fail.
Let go of any regrets
Over things you've done and said.
You can't go back in time,
So let go of the what if's and should have's
That are in your mind.
Let go of bad thoughts about yourself
And the comparison to someone else.
Let go of the hurt from those who did you wrong
And all the criticism you get,
Let it be gone.
Let it all go.
It's okay to do so.

Kathy Renee Krzewinski
Chattanooga, TN

Finding Recovery

Six steps in my heart
To the promised land

One
Day
At
A
Time
Love

And she drinks it in
Sometimes hungrily,
And sometimes
with a brokenness.
Passing over her eyes

Is a silver cloud,
And dripping are her days
From the blessing of her brow

I move on
An echo louder than myself,
In summer rainstorms.

Rena E. Kerchner
Silver Spring, MD

Moonlit Reminders

Midnight sings her song
Stirring the wilder things
I hear the soft tears of a moonlit sky
"Why are you weeping?"
I ask, gazing at the stars
Sparkling like freckles on a beautiful face
"You are so beautiful, my earth"
She speaks softly,
A gentle breeze careens as a lullaby
Over the night stricken land
"So beautiful, but content to hate yourself"
A tear falls
Shimmering in the midnight sky
"Can you not see by the light I give you?
Can you not see that as dark as it may be,
I will always be here to light
Your darkest night
And bring sparkles
To the darkest of dreams."

Dani Strong
Mitchell, SD

Suppose

I should suppose, poets cherish gardens
where a seed, nurtured and properly loved
blooms into all things beautiful and right—
a crafty metaphor for life and verse.
I am supposed, I should suppose, to love
all flavors of sage flowers and fauna,
everything from forsythia to ferns.
But, I am frail and falter, I suppose.
So today, my back ached from long hours
of digging through and around stubborn roots,
planting orderly rows of Columbines
and Hostas, clawing in black muck and mud.
I saw crawling earthworms enough to know—
Gravid soil teemed with black-rot riches
An earthy oasis—decay and dirt,
the fruits of my labor firmly rooted.
We all will be harvested all too soon,
uprooted only to be planted one
last time. Short lived mayflies one and all.
Till we too are sown deep in muck and mud.
I rubbed my eyes with hands rolled in wet soil
mulling over when I too am worm food—
buried deep, deep into dark dirt. Aren't we
all waiting to celebrate death? I suppose.

Peter L. Shaheen
Bloomfield, MI

The Color I've Become

If everything I've ever known
resides in the past
as some ill-colored kaleidoscope
of fog I can't reclaim,
then I cannot possibly know who I am today.
Similarly, if what's to come is unknown,
but brighter than what was,
I guess the future's a faded pastel,
lacking the direction to point me where to go.
Unable to bridge connections,
I'm sitting in the present,
slapping palettes together,
and without reference of transitions,
my efforts merge into a repugnant brown.
Brown becomes me,
and I become it.
We sit together and reminisce;
we sit and wait for something that ceases to exist.
And until I can reclaim
what once was
I am unidentifiable
murky
lost outside the color wheel.

Kim Rosinsky
Conway, AR

Shorter Farmer

A hungover farmer went one day
To a blacksmith's shop to buy some hay.
Well dear reader this isn't funny
For you see he had no money,
And so went home less vertebrae.

Richard Breese
San Francisco, CA

Lover's Cross

I know that my love for you
Will not...or cannot
Be as I had hoped it could be
I know that our friendship is something special
Something that few ever find
My heart yearns to spend all of eternity with you
But if this is all that is fated to be
There is nothing I can do
But bear this lover's cross for you
Please don't think less of me because
My shoulders are able to carry the weight
Until the world ends
And I know that I am the luckiest
And most blessed man to ever have lived

Thomas Edward Platz
Akron, OH

In the End

From start to finish,
There is always an end.
From birth to death,
There is always an end.
Even in words, like friend.
There is always an end.
Do you see? the end,
let's forget about that,
We want the beginning.
Let's start something new,
I feel something starting to brew.
But there is always something,
A bump in the road, a dead end.
Look at that, it's back,
The ending of a road.
But keep hope, and look ahead.
Seeing a light, could be the start,
Of a bad ending.
In the end we all suffer,
But eventually we all subside.
I'm in this for the long ride,
No near ending's for me.
In the end,
I am here.

Randi Lynn Stewart
Buffalo, NY

Senseless Malapropisms

My ears shatter when I hear you staring.
I can feel your footsteps
as they break my heart.
My eyes melt
as if that cherry pie is the culprit.
Wishful thinking
only draws our toes in the sand.
A line that crosses
what we outsource as normal.
I taste like I've been playing the piano.
The best flavor of jazz you know?
And how do you know?
There are notes that you should
maybe take down on your
heart on your sleeve.
Sleeveless dresses dress to impress.
Impress the interviewees who
don't do much with their time.
Time is of the essence, but the essence is imaginary.
Time is a construct.
Construct a new world; world of thought.
Thought you ought to know
know thyself better.
Better off dead than dead to me.

Rachel Ellynn M.
Kansas City, MO

The Dirt Doctor

There once was a very special lady.
She had a talent that transcended life.
Dirt was an enemy she fought daily.
And she earned the title of housewife.

She could eyeball a tiny speck moving
From twenty yards away to say the least.
Before you knew it, she'd take off zooming
Right next to the spot and it was deceased.

A blower, vacuum and dust pan are tools
That our heroine uses all through the day.
She's on the alert and lays out the rules.
If dirt is around, stay out of her way.

Doctor she'd be if there was a degree
Because housecleaning is her specialty.

Shelly J. Darlow
Sarasota, FL

Jumping Through Life

I jumped so high once before
that I know life ain't true, so believe me,
I know what life can put you through,
So I'm pretty sure you'll know what I'm saying to you!
It's not like I refuse to go through,
But there are some things in life,
You can't do! Believe me,
I know no matter how high you jump,
Life it just ain't true,
So my advice for you,
Don't listen to a fool,
Jump around where you just might get through,
Believe me it's not an easy thing to do,
No matter what you do,
Just know that the fool isn't you,
Just know that you go through!

Travis Anthony Larson
Lakeside, CA

The Magic Within Myself

I was born with a soul to sensitive to cold,
I felt things deeper than most,
I have a wandering mindless wakes,
I get excited about the changes of the seasons ,
The sound of the ocean,
The smell of the rain,
The starry night & warm sunsets,
The universe fell in love with the stubborn heart,
Magic happens when you don't give up,
Realize your not the same person you use to be,
Your lights back on & shine it better than ever.

Tiffany Evans
Tracy, CA

Voices from the Lord

I will sing praises to you my lord if you give me the voice of the river, that wondrous flowing that only you could have made.
I will sing above all other noise if you give me the voice of the mighty wind, whose twists and turns cut like a blade.
I will sing ever so loud if you give me the voice of the ocean, with the waters of their mighty great fall
I will sing out most beautiful if you give me the voice of an angel, this voice is most precious above all.

Teresa O. Gates
Thomasville, AL

Not White

Look at me
Look at my skin
Can't you see this beautiful brown?
From head to toe all this melanin
A white woman in disguise?
That doesn't sound sensible to me
I'm clearly a strong black woman
Clearly for those who can truly see
No I'm not ghetto
I'm rarely ever loud
A walking Oreo, how?
Because I choose not to hang with ignorant crowds
I speak properly
I love to annunciate every word
Oh what a black woman can't be educated?
That's completely and utterly absurd
I wear glasses, stay in the library
I'm a classic "teachers pet"
You may laugh now, but later
You'll soon regret
I don't care for the "wave"
I do my own thing
See I'm not white
There's power in my skin
Power from generations before me
Power I'll pass to my next of kin

Tiana M. Bowers
Utica, NY

Why Poetry

To make each moment
an eternity;
To see the holy
in a grain of sand;
To turn the simple
in to the profound;
Lighten the shadows
and darken the flame;
Contrast the daylight of
cool moonlit bays;
Bring forth the mystery
lying within;
Bring out the essence of
objective truth

Sonja Stalnaker
Lake Stevens, WA

Unknown

Lost in thought and consumed with fear,
Feelings of angst suddenly appear.
Fine on the outside,
Colorful and bright.
But who am I really?
Just a girl lost in the fight.

Rebecca Parsons
Springfield, MO

Arrival

The day that has been predestined has come to me with a warning.
My strength is my weakness.
A truth which no one can deter.
I have come to the end of my journey.
A call to the lost of this world.

I have seen the youth of today.
The crush of their souls that they initiate.
They have no direction...
lacking compassion.
Everyday they should ask....

"How can I change the world?"
"How can I leave a mark?"

Should I use my body as a canvas or express my words as graffiti.
A message in a bottle.
A bottle that was tossed on the first day of arrival.
No glory or fame.
Only to sustain.
Eagerly awaiting the call to proclaim.

That to live is to die to envy!
To walk the paths least taken.
A life is full of mystery when the tears that you shed will help create your
history.

Make no promises that you can't achieve just push forward and set
yourself free.

Alejandro Noel Garza
San Antonio, TX

Elysian Fields

All was lost
I was defenseless,
Then I saw it
The Elysian Fields so endless.
A tearful ending
In exchange for beauty,
To be offered a gift like this
When I wasn't even ready.
Fields of wheat I see
Lightly grazing the flowers,
Walking ever so slowly
I understand its true power.
Warm and cool tones of light
Are all I observe for miles,
Nothing but shades of gold
To make me smile.
Comforting angelic hymns
Surround my sensitive ears,
As a gentle harp rings free
A wonderful sound to hear.
And right before my eyes
Comes a bright man,
Rays of blinding light
Emitting and covering the land.
Welcome home he said
As i embraced him,
Under his breath whispered
Son and my chances were now slim.
My father was a sight to behold
Seems paradise is real,
Because I never knew
Until I entered the fields.

Nick James Nguyen
Lafayette, CA

Coffee House Soundtrack

Sometimes I feel like one of those teapots you fill from the top and pour
into the cup below,
so it's seemingly endless.
My soul pouring out,
hoping there's something there to catch it,
fill something up with warm word vomit.
Sometimes I can't stop myself and I'll spend 3 minutes with someone
before letting them know
I'm a Gemini and I don't get along with Libras;
That I teach yoga, follow the moon cycles,
And there are probably some small childhood traumas I haven't worked
out.
My brain is filled with useless knowledge and fun facts,
like the fax machine has been around longer than the telephone.
I can memorize a song after listening to it maybe 3 times,
so I can sing along with any artist I follow on Spotify,
but I can't add without using my fingers.
Sometimes I feel like I wasn't put together right,
or that this isn't how I picture myself,
or that my body doesn't always feel like mine.
Like, maybe, this vessel was something or someone else, simply serving it's
purpose now.
Like, maybe, comments over time from strangers and close friends
has made me distance myself from myself and say
"here, you deal with it."
Sometimes my teapot overflows,
and when I pour it out,
I just hope there's something there to catch it.

Adare Toral
San Luis Obispo, CA

Memory Lost

Daddy are you there?
Maybe he can't hear me
I feel your despair
know you want to be free
Feel that you're letting go
I beg you to keep on
Love you more than you know
I beg you to stay strong
I know it's hard
Wondering why
Can't control what leaves you scarred
Hurts my heart to see you cry
I know it's confusing
I feel your pain
Your life is now an illusion
Slipping into insane
Wait, what?
Daddy are you there?

Tess Baker
Mechanicsburg, PA

Drowning in Love

My lungs fill with water
the longer I'm under.
My eyes remain closed,
to avoid seeing what's ahead.
My hands feel around me,
seeking a way out.

However, there isn't one.
So, I opened my eyes.
I realized there's no water
and I was drowning
in my love for you.

Trisha DaBolt
Hamburg, NY

Nurturing Hand

The sun shines through the window
The rusted glass has been broken
Your presence awakens the forgotten home
You clean up the broken glass
Painting the old bricks yellow
Nurturing me
Almost like a sign from God
I unfold into your hands like sand

Lejla Mecavica
Mishawaka, IN

The Tree

A tree stood tall and firm in the ground.
It's been here since the beginning of time,
Witness men destroy each other countless times.
Why was this tree still there?

Standing firm and staring into the abyss.
Men from the world came to see
The longevity of this steady tree.
Why was this tree still there?

A voice uttered from the stem
My purpose in life has been to watch you grow.
When you reached you lowest,
I would be there to give you hope.

When you lost faith in one another,
Turn against each other
Brewed hate among the feathers
I would be there to lift up your soul.
I would be there to help you grow.

Because I am the tree of life,
Filled with history in sight
To be man's guidance to light.
I am but mere a tree,
To teach you a lesson about life

This is why I am still here!

Yehuwdiyth Yodhhewawhe
Celebration, FL

Early Mornings

Spend some time with me and watch the dawn break.
Linger a while longer, and to me cling.
Let it all collide and watch the world wake

Your heart slows down with each slow breath you take
Your smile still shines as the daffodils sing
Spend some time with me and watch the dawn break.

With each sun ray, our slumber seems to break.
We watch as the wind blows and trees take wing.
Let it all collide and watch the world wake.

Settle down to hear the sounds wild birds make
as new beginnings make our bare souls ring.
Spend some time with me and watch the dawn break.

I ask for this, but only for your sake,
because you need to learn to enjoy spring.
Let it all collide and watch the world wake.

The morning soon brings end to all our ache
Our time has come - our future in full fling.
Spend some time with me and watch the dawn break.
Let it all collide and watch the world wake.

Xiomara Michelle Martinez Alejandro
San Antonio, TX

Mourning

Death doesn't come at a convenient time
like a period at the end of a sentence,
the amen at the end of a prayer,
or the bell at the end of class.
It drops in on you unexpectedly
while you are eating or watching a movie,
an unwelcome guest
for which there was no seat at the table,
a power outage that turns off all your lights
and ends your existence on this plane
to the dismay of those who loved you
and wanted to have another chance to tell you.

Death doesn't walk a straight line
or stand mute like a solid brick wall.
It zigzags and dances at your wake
allowing you a brief glimpse of the mourners
assembled in celebration of your life
before taking you across the rainbow to eternity.

Death doesn't mourn or grieve,
no tears of sorrow from the great beyond.
The reaper separates the wheat from the chaff
freeing your soul from its earthbound shackle
and letting you soar free and undefined.

Death doesn't recall your moments of joy or sadness.
Nor does it place your life on a scale
to sing your praises or bemoan your failures.
It opens the pores of your being
to allow your essence to mix with the ether.

Jay Frankston
Little River, CA

Hearing the Blues

When some women hear blues
inside honky tonk bar
They kick off their high heels
hold them over their shoulder
Bare foot now older and bolder
inside they go finding a place to deal
with way blues makes them feel

No forgetting can hide
the way blues sway you away inside
to where reason to care
for love was once so much a thrill to share
But then music slides sharp
and you sink into Blues coming on bad
thinking about gone wrong love you once had

William Joe Pyles
Fair Grove, MO

Colors of the Morning

I will not cry for you
For you live in the colors of the morning.
You run with the river,
And you breathe with the wind.
You are here forever
But without suffering or pain.
You are where you need to be,
And so I will not cry for me.

Sophia Singh
Yardley, PA

Death Be Love

I was afraid of Death, but then I met Him.
And he showed me all that I might miss.
Somehow, I believe he thought to save me.
There was something so familiar in his kiss.
I know I loved him, and his promise.
I tried so hard to be his all.
But I understood in time, that love was cold.
And then I heard a more compelling call.
I turned to tell him that I loved him.
He had already turned away.
But in that moment of deepest sorrow;
I learned to live another day.

Sherry Godfrey
Cincinnati, OH

Recovery

I apologize to the one that now
   Wants to hold my delicate heart.
I am sorry if it turns to ashes before your eyes.
I apologize if my hugs feel like a thorn bush.
I apologize if my kisses are antifreeze.
I apologize for cringing, over thinking,
   for every time I revert.
I apologize for talking about this so much,
It must be tiring to listen to the same song again.

And I thank you.
For being so willing to burn up with me
   As I walk through the fires of my memory.
For being the concrete barriers I drive into
   When my brain turns to squirming maggots
   That can only repeat the same thought.
For learning to crush those maggot thoughts
   When you assure me that my life is changing.
That this time I am enough.
For being able to soothe my trembling bones
   As I begin to recover my own flesh
   From the mouth of the hungry wolf.
For not being another wolf.

Victoria Cipriana Valenzuela
El Paso, TX

A Broken Image

I am a puppet.
Controlled by the standards built around me.
The expectations written all over me.
And the words that hit deep within me.
I am not me.
Just a mirror of what everyone expects me to be.
Just another image of how they perceive me.
Just another empty glass to break.
A broken image.
I am someone I have made myself into a long time ago.
I am someone I don't want to be.
But the person everyone expects me to be.
I am a puppet.
Another shared image of everyone's expectations.
Except for my owns.

Victoire Onokoko
Houston, TX

I Can Dream

I can't sing, but I can dream,
of a place,
where there is no war,
killing no more.
Where people love and not hate.
Where there isn't greed,
People succeed.
Its sad to say,
I'm part of this human race.
Where people lie, kill and steal,
because of their free will.
Riots gangs, and such,
Life doesn't matter much.
War is real, peace won't come,
It looks like Satan has won.
In this world there is strife,
Someday soon we will
 have a better life.
Until then, watch and pray,
til God comes down,
and takes us away.

Valerie Ann Gammon
Mercer, PA

Time Is Moving Fast

time to be your Father
time to come running when you start crying
bring the bottle with me because you are starving

you are growing up now, you have started to crawl
now you're everywhere
you are no longer small

you tried to crawl up the wall
you ended up standing tall
knowing you do not have balance
I put a pillow to ease your fall

you are walking around
you turned the house into your playground, your toys everywhere
I would ask you to pick it up, but in my eyes
you are still my baby girl

you have started school
you waved me goodbye and you said "I love you too"
but it is not enough for me
I still feel like I'm losing you
before you know it you will fall in love
and I will not be the one in your heart
but you will always be in mine
throughout time

Veronica Nneoma Okafor
Grand Prairie, TX

Land of the Free

We are living in a world that locks away the addicts
The government gets you addicted then criminalizes the habit
College graduates can't even get work yet they arrest you when you slang,
Acting like you can feed your kids and pay rent with spare change

The war in the east spread like mange and please tell me what was solved?
Countless deaths, children's tears will we ever evolve? Homeless vets are
dying right here on our own soil.

The true war is government against citizen and you don't matter if you're
not as rich as royals, they send you over to fight their battle just for you
to survive and die at home, they have the power to save you but you leave
this world alone

Clones in MAGA hats screaming build a wall while the real threat is
sitting in the white house safe watching his country fall,
Call on the protesters to fight for the rights of a fetus
yet when a dying Syrian child begs for help they turn their backs and say
refugees aren't loved by their jesus

Please believe us when we say there's no end in sight, they pass these beliefs
to the next generation and the darkness outweighs any light ...

Amanda Merriman
Muskogee, OK

I Am a Lotus

I am a lotus, born in muddy waters
Rising to the surface, radiating purity
Floating in serenity, concealed at night
Beautified bravery despite adversity
Each day creating my own destiny.

I am a lotus, a warrior cloaked queen
Rising to the surface, soaking wet
Washed clean, freedom to dream
Shielded in passion, dodging fears
Beautified growth in strained tears
Each day preparing my own survival.

I am a lotus, a lover thief of hearts
Rising to the surface, convicted of charm
Burning desire, simmering embers
Blind sincerity, giver of hugs
Beautified healer in confidence and love
Each day planting my own kindness.

I am a lotus, a friend that's true
Rising to the surface, defining purpose
Seeping loyalty, acceptance of you
Vibrantly humorous, spreading joy
Beautified character in seasoned bloom
Each day fighting my own gloom
Savoring blessings and fiery souls
I am a lotus, letting my strength and imperfections unfold.

Stephanie Marie Lewis
Lamoine, ME

A Dark Place

A dark place has noises, sounds, & voices
It makes me question, what are my choices?
Shall I choose death or shall I choose life?
Figures of an angel & a demon, one pointing to the dark, one pointing to the light

A dark place is tears running down my cheek
It's suffering in silence, so afraid to speak
It's being ashamed of my sadness, being all in my head
Laying down late at night, wishing I was dead

A dark place is heavy, like a thousand bricks
Mind game after mind game, trick after trick
& the taste, oh it's bitter it's never sweet
Leaves me feeling dirty & ugly, no sense of complete

A dark place is quiet, only my thoughts to be heard
Trapped in I am, like a Petco bird
Chirping away, I gnaw at the cage
Unable to escape & it feels so strange

But oh murky dark place, what if I told you you're just all in my head?
Would my resilience be a bother & threaten your stead?
A dark place I'm fighting you & I hope you're afraid
I'm sorry dark place, but here I shan't stay

Sophia Joy Russo
Scottsdale, AZ

Letter to Arene

I never used to believe in love at first sight,
But after you eyes met mine I was lost,
Lost in deep brown windows into an abyss.
I was drowning without putting up a fight,
Submerged into your soul sealed with a kiss.
Every second after we first met
I knew it was you that my heart has be yearning for.
The days went by,
and as I listened to your mix tapes
my eyes would smile as I'd turn up the dial.
Falling in love with you was like falling in love for the first time.
Falling in love with you was like feeling alive for the first time.
Some people would say I got lucky,
but I got blessed.
Arene you're my world,
You got me to write again.
You Took a simple man and taught him convolution.
It's a prayer answered hallelujah amen.
You took a broken man lost in destitution,
Someone who needed a life to begin.
Even on our worst days I know I have you by my side.
And when I mess up please know that I tried,
Tried to give you everything I got.
Cause this love was never an afterthought.

Christian Charles Kubie
Ellsworth AFB, SD

The Soldier

He is there today in his dark place, of the old him there is no trace
it is a day of mood and gloom, you can feel it in every inch of the room
it is because of his life as a soldier
A time when he was hard and much bolder
He was trained to be tough, strong and brave
No one told him of the memories that would go with him to his grave
The flashbacks that come out of no where
The days he only makes it by a prayer
The things he has seen, the things he has done
Most mere men would turn around and run
The ghost that visit his mind; their fate intertwined
The memories he would like to forget
Some that cause him to pop out in a sweat
People feel like they understand
But can they really? They never wore the boots of this man
The many things that are put on paper or represented by a pin
Only tell a portion of where this soldier has been
The war he served in was over fast
The impact of those days will last and last
He saw grown men cry; watching a friend, another soldier die
You'll never know the suffering and pain
You just know that some days the heartache and memories reign
For freedom and liberty he will always fight
As a soldier he knows that is what's right!

Shirley J. Flowers
Kirksville, MO

Slow Down

Take the time to look around you.
There is so much beauty to see.
Don't be in such a hurry to see the day end, and night enter.
Enjoy each day, and treat it like a gift that is given to you.
Appreciate what life has to offer.
Move forward with your life, because only you can reach your goals.
Time goes by so fast, and we are left with memories.
Take the time to appreciate the world around you.

Linda Lee Calabrese
New Milford, CT

Black Mentality

Numb to the sirens outside my window frame,
if these four walls could talk it would reveal my deepest pain.
Each day I walk outside I step outside my comfort zone,
in a world full of people but my soul's on its own.
Stuck in the cycle of the black mentality,
all I wanna do is love but survival is the key.
A dog eat dog world 'cause we want the same things,
and swear it was luck when we grabbing at our dreams.

Iisha Taylor
Louisville, KY

A Prison of Your Own Making

Time: shackles holding us back,
Unfelt by the child, bearing down on the adult.
An accumulating mass leaving nothing,
No room to imagine, to indulge - merely air to breathe.
Reality takes hold with no way to fight it off,
Merely stand your ground.
How?
Build a wall, wear a mask.
No gate, no exit, no risk of exposure.
That's the goal, is it not?
A wall that began as a protective barrier
Becomes a fortress - invulnerable, impregnable.
A mask once a shield takes on an identity of its own,
Its own personality, its own agenda.
Their mission: keep you safe.
Safe from what?
Translation: to keep you restrained.
Whispers telling you what to do,
How to act, who to love.
The gentle nudges, by themselves, inconsequential,
Together, the defining elements of the puppet master
Taking the reins and not letting go anytime soon.
Isolation makes its own claim to the throne.
Time, Fear, Isolation …
We've got ourselves a party,
And you're the congenial host.

Sara Alexandra Taylor
Beaverton, OR

Twelve

He'll change,
She hoped....

He didn't.

"Please stay,"
He spoke...

She didn't.

Kyle Bong
Yucca valley, CA

Mirabile

On a winter day 'midst a crowd of people
Rose two white doves from St. Peter's steeple,
As the Pope said a prayer for peace on earth
For the hearts' redemption and the souls' rebirth.
And the birds flew skyward with a gentle flutter
As the crowd commenced to buzz and mutter,
For a crow and a gull attacked each dove
Like aircraft battling in the skies above.
The peace doves shining in the morning light
Struck the crow and gull as just too darn white.
And the Pope's head bowed as the doves flew east
And the crowd broke up for their Sunday feast.

Stephen Fournier
Hartford, CT

Threats of Promise

Who's stupid enough to believe
That love is a finite fantasy
Dedicated to only good?
It's fuel for the fear it conceives
Mere threats to consume in secrecy
I wish it would

If all the contributing factors
Lay claim to what we're after
then who can say
That liberation isn't a matter
Of the Ever-needed disasters
From our dismay?

All the vows that are required
To uphold such shallow desires
Do make our love innate
Often times I'm deeply inspired
By our minds that do conspire
To clash with fate

Ill never let you go.

Jessica Stevens
St. Charles, MO

Degrees of Worrying

I saw my dad worrying about many things in life
like losing my mom to any sudden health issue
or for me to find a good groom for marriage...
He constantly 2nd guessed his parenting skills.
Besides us, I heard him disclose to his buds,
The other worries from his heart and mind,
when he thought I wasn't listening or old
to understand that most men stress too
about the same things that women do
like their figure, skin, scars and hair...
On philosophical discussions, I heard,
that he also worried about - balding
and not finding a job, if terminated.
Or being able to perform in bed -
after a certain age, of course...
Funnily enough, he told me...
That he sometimes worried
about being locked alone
accidentally in the room.
I was confused to know,
that he was conscious-
of a few stretch marks,
behind both his knees.
Amazingly, he didn't
ever worry about...
life or the sudden
accident that
ended all his
worries.

Sunayna Pal
Rockville, MD

The Boy

The boy
With leather jackets
And skinny jeans.
The boy
With heavy cologne
To mask the cigarettes.
The boy
With pretty blue eyes
And a half crooked smile.
The boy
Whispering beautiful lies
And spending every lonely night.
Don't fall for his pretty face-
There's deadly intentions.
The devil isn't dressed in horns
On a throne of lost souls,
He's everything you want
Behind a pretty boy's smile.

Summerlynn Marie Turner
Bowling Green, KY

A Romantic Interlude

from my lips feathery kisses
on my life line's sun kissed tresses
child like eyes filling with warmth
cherub cheeks robust and rosy
my core alights my place, my hearth
sweet planes shiver with my caress
my paradise, candied silkiness
velvet fields I now uncover
my hands glide slow on my temptress
deafening pulses from lovers

Samantha DeWitt
Lakewood, WA

The Loneliest Child

I covet the isolation that I find inside my room.
Bathed in utter loneliness and swathed in utter gloom.
Why do I hold the darkness and emptiness inside.
I seek a place to cry in, where feelings I can hide.

So let me go into my room don't try to hold my hand.
There's something troubling in in my life, you wouldn't understand.

Alone with my thoughts and feelings is something I can't resist
So walk away and just pretend I never did exist.

Susan C. Daugherty
Branchport, NY

Don't Waste Time

Fog rolls over the turquoise water
Oceans rise and fall in a rhythm real and magical
Sounds of a heartbeat in tune with gravity of the earth
Sun peeks through mist and cretes a sensation of delight
I wonder what this life here is really like
A universe of wonders twirling around in space
A miniscule object of being with no guidance or face
Creation and thought occupy my delirious mind
In the end hoping that God will be kind
Allow me the pleasure of roaming in fantasy
Delighting my senses with untold ecstasy
With one there is so much compassion
During daily flight of untold passion
Longing to be in a connection of time
Hear me you all who are so devine
This life is short so don't waste time.

Susan Kaufman
Sunny Isles Beach, FL

Crime Scene

She paints the picture a brighter green,
With trees and flowers consuming the scene.
The sky is bright and the air is cool,
While the legs still wiggle on a high seat stool.

Still thinking positive ideas with lighter thought,
While she enjoys the food she just had bought.
The home is silent and her mood is calm,
With just the brush in her palm.

Calmness has managed to subdue the flare,
Of a predator lurking with an evil stare.
Still stuck in a world that doesn't care,
She makes a ponytail of her hair.

Although the reality isn't bright,
She keeps what's positive in her sight.
She pushes the darkness to the side,
When the door unexpectedly opens wide.

She gets surprised by a familiar mass,
As she knocks a potter with flattened glass.
To fast to even feel,
He's the rope and she's the reel.

He didn't give time for a conscience to work,
He maintained the trance in the hour lurk.
She was able to scream out loud,
But neighbors are useless, without a crowd.

Kristie Anne Raccuglia
Marco Island, FL

Stolen Hearts, Broken Souls

my heart was stolen from my chest
by a girl with willowy arms and a broken soul
whose spidery fingers grasped my mind
a puppeteer she became to me
leaving only darkness in this pitch black world
her rail legs sitting on the earth
round and round it turns
slowly fading away
leaving dust as the only existence to stay

Lorelai Madison Symmes
Millersville, MD

Why?

Why?
He held me close
Our hearts beating as one
Touching our bodies
Passion flowing
Both of us knowing
But neither of us knowing
Where the other is going
Passion high
Now we know why
This thing called love
Can make us high
And again we ask ourselves
Why?
Why is this thing called LIFE!

Kristan E. Elkins
Detroit, MI

Her Time to Shine

She is strong, she is brave
She is resilient, she is fire
She may bend but never break
She may cry but refuse to back down
She is strength, she stands her ground
She is a protector, she is fierce
She carries herself with grace
She will calmly face adversity
She will go the distance whatever it takes
She is a warrior
She stands tall and proud
Her time to shine is now

Kristy D. Beason
Oxford, AL

Search for Prosperity

I've felt betrayed by my own sanity
Forgetting myself on a search for prosperity
My shame, my pain, my everlasting heartbreak
If I had listened to my conscious,
Then maybe my heart would have stayed protected
I spaced and left my protection
Hands that were so welcoming became a rejection
I've forgotten who I was
Gave up my past for a reality
A reality only found in insanity
On this search for prosperity

Blossom Lovekill
Lexington, GA

Daylight

When the morning rise above
the heavenly kingdom,
the flowers awake
from their slumber
The leaves of life bloom as
rose and stand strong
above the Garden of Eden.

The daylight has come
to awake the nature world
The grass brights it's color
green and turn into pale
when nightlight comes.

The roses bright its color
red and turn into blood
when nightlight comes
The sunflowers roam over
the Garden of Eden and
bright it's color yellow and
turn into greyish- orange
when the nightlight comes.

The daylight has come
to spread its beautiful of
glory and delight
Beware it cannot be taken
or present into the world
of sins.

Daisy Sarah Ray Sunflowers
Temple, TX

Time to Move Forward

I speak and no one hears the words that I say
I listen to you I did so today
I laugh out loud while alone with a thought
I cry deep within feeling lost and distraught.
I remember the rough roads that I have traveled
I also remember the wars I have battled
I've been up and I've been down
oftentimes I wore a frown
the end of that was the beginning of this
it started with a hug and finished with a kiss
time to move forward I've been stuck for way too long
time to admit the things I've done wrong
next time I talk will you listen not just hear?
Undivided attention lend me an ear
My words are not always easy to understand
but this is my life No Fantasyland
we are two separate people United as one
the love that we share can never be undone

Krystal Dunning
Lakeland, FL

Beautiful Soul

Her soul?
Beautiful
Her voice?
Magical
Her impact on people's lives?
Indescribable
The kind of person who was easy
To love
The kind of person
Who you always fell in love with
A beautiful soul indeed
Took my breath away
With each sentence she spoke
Swept me off my feet with her beauty
A beautiful soul who lost her life
A beautiful soul whose dreams will not
Be fulfilled
A beautiful soul
Whose heart is no longer beating
A beautiful soul whose voice
Will be no longer heard
Her beautiful soul
Is put at rest
I love you meu amor
I will see you on the other side

Kirsten Louise Albis
Holbrook, MA

In a Den of Poets

hello again,
my age old friend the canvas of my mind
As I often do,
I turn to you,
In hopes that I shall find
An escape for the sheltered voice
Shaken and deprived of choice
Confined to chains of fear so deep
It never dared to take the leap
But tonight,
As each of them took their place
I craved for the freedom upon their face
For with each layer of soul revealed
I longed to know the magic, the feel
The release of the madness and passion
To grieve and rejoice with adjoined compassion
My pallet of perception became more driven
By contemplations of creation unwritten
Inspired, perhaps conspired by words
Not merely listened to but heard
Flowing through the broken and lifted
As words are envisioned by the guide of the gifted
Reaching out through the unteaching of time
Touched by expressions more moving than rhyme
For the rhythms that were carried off of their hearts
Are what gave life and divinity to their art
Oh how I long for even the briefest taste
To feel that very freedom upon my face

Kira Anne Cwalina
Folsom, PA

Intertwined

Your scent is on my clothes.
Your memories linger in my room.
Your shadow falls upon my bed.
Your hair clogs my drain.
Your air fills my lungs.
Your pain smolders in my heart.
How could you leave me with so much, yet so little?

Matt Strauch
Mechanicsburg, PA

The Little Girl in Me

Someone asked me what are you running from?
I said that little girl and me that is screaming depression.
I mean she won't let me sleep and life is feeling restless
so I guess it's time to have that talk, maybe make a confession.
I said *why are you here?* She said *you tell me why are you lost?*
So now I'm talking to myself feeling crazy.
She said *I'm you, you me so stop acting shady and tell me why you played me.*
I didn't but you did, out here living a lie
trying to make friends faking a smile
you forgot about me the girl that lay within
I was trying to be your friend
Why are you running from our past?
This is all your fault—here goes depression again.
Now everything is coming back up and you starting to get stuck
and this is all because you didn't stop to work on us.
Let's take a break, let's take a breather and stop right here.
Pause—this conversation is to be continued

Kierra Nicole Deloch
Saint Louis, MO

False Heart

Feelings don't come from the heart
Because if the heart is in my left side
Why does it always hurt in the center?
My heart beats five score and ten,
While the phantom inside my chest
Gushes river of tears
Like a lady dressed in rags bleeding from a hundred wounds
Tearing apart her hair.
Wherein comes this sadness,
punching a hole through my lungs?
It cannot be from my heart,
my good friend, who gives me life
Feeling comes from the soul,
languishing in its fifth chamber as it tears me apart from the inside.
Happiness is it's only solace, scarcer than a four leaf clover
But still, it is better to feel sorrow
For nothing is worse than feeling dead inside.

Sumaya Khoshnobish
Elmhurst, NY

Vinyl Record

To me her love was more than just "love"
To me the way she loved was a record.
A sensuous pin in the groove.
And when she'd speak she'd spin around and around.
To me that was all that mattered.
I danced in her rhythm.
Finding it impossible to deny what was evident.
In a mere matter of moments I was enticed.
Tracing the lines of her hands,
I being the pin lost in her melatonin.
Whether in public for all to see.
Or in the intimate moments shared between her and I.
I sung her love as my favorite song.
A song forever engraved as I longed to be the pin
that traced her groove.
A record that always stays with you
No matter how much time has passed

Kewayne Wadley
Memphis, TN

Wondering Me

I wake up and wonder what to do
Same room, but still seems new
Adventure, just how to achieve
Upper echelons, and who to relieve

So many beliefs, so much success
How does the universe choose whom to bless?
Evolution, character, do let me know
I'm afraid soon I won't be able to bend down low

Until then,

Watching the stars, obeying the sun
Writing a poem, quipping a pun
These little distractions pass the time
Though have not fed the mouths of these friends of mine

So, if you can fit one more at that table of yours
Pray, let me sit, I'll soon leave back out your doors
Then let me experience such a life
Providing all offered to my wife

Anthony Brian Mallgren
Bronx, NY

Behind the Smile

I wish you could see the pain in my eyes,
The smile that covers it up creating self depleting lies.
I wish the shattered pieces of my heart were able to be pieced whole
heartedly back together,
But the devastating pain I endure is a lethal emotion I'll end up feeling
forever.
If only the happiness I felt when I was with you was a feeling guaranteed
to last,
But I suffer from trauma and I pushed you away because of my past.
Why is what you ask, but the answer is unknown,
No matter how close you get and safe you make me feel I will continue to
feel alone.
I pushed you away because I was scared of the fact that someone actually
cared,
But it was nothing but our love for each other that was mending my
broken heart and creating a heart that was repaired.
Love is a mystery that you helped me begin to solve,
But like putting an acidic object in liquid my faith slowly dissolved.
I wish I could say I know why I continue to push the one thing I love more
than anything away,
But as if it were a museum my heart is only shortly on display.
Everyone seems to want it but it's a simple you cannot have,
It's a rare piece of art that originally is only created once but is based upon
a deep dark path.
I know one thing that has been hiding and my heart longs to share,
My heart is a fire and the love you so genuinely placed me before caused
an unthinkable radioactive flare.

Lena Rose Rounds
Tell City, IN

A.K.A Love

From the moment i met you
Till the day that you died
Said your name was love
Should've known that you lied
Love would never beat
A heart so defenseless
Toss it on shelves
Or leave it on fences
Love would never hurt
A heart that was pure
Like the way you did
Why love? What for?
What did the heart do
To make love so rotten
Could it be from it's past
And never forgotten
The heart never wanted
To play in love's game
It's one goal in life
Was to know love's real name

Lee Klareich
Oldsmar, FL

Tears

I was in your womb growing and feeling
love and compassion.
when you pushed me out, I looked into
your beautiful eyes and I knew that you love
Me.
when I was a toddler and fell you pick me up
and kiss my forehead
when I was a teenager and became a woman for the
first time you gave me a hug.
when I became a parent for the first time and smile you
said, baby I am proud of you.
when my dad passed away you look into my eyes and
said it was going to okay
When I had my heart broken for the first time, you cried
with me until I fell asleep
When I bought my car for the first time, you co-sign
and encourage me to drive.
When my boyfriend was beating on me
you came to my rescue and stay with me in
the hospital.
The doctors told me that I have short-term of
memory loss, but you never left my side
They say you need two parents to complete a family
but you stay strong for me
When my dad left and you saw me crying
you grab me and said you always have mommy.

Lavette Gibson
College Park, GA

Charity Case

We fell in love, I got ill
Your love disappeared
I'm nothing ,you are something
We said I Do's, with my enemy you are cool
Value me protect me, please have my back
Protect my emotions throughout the storm
How can you be so calm?
Drama is causing my heart pain
Walk away let's not become estranged
You don't want me but I need you
You're around because I'm sick
If I was healed you wouldn't be here
Feel pity, feel sorry, feel love acting Godly
Saved me, continued distress you're the devil in the midst of the mess
Feeling less than, want to be more than I use to be
Found my own way, Poetry gives me light
No more using what you've done for me to make yourself feel right

Brittany Lakkia Woods
Murfreesboro, TN

Last Day of School

Morning rush and breakfast is a flurry
A sip of something, bite of toast, all in a hurry
Homework's done, as usual, just barely
Forgot to kiss mom and dad left so early
Packed my lunch to save some money
Rode the bus, laughed at nothing funny
Homeroom chatter, discussing lunch and snaps
Fire alarm pulled, teachers walking into traps
Heard the shots and screams from the hall
Hid under the desk, on my phone, tried to call
Help is on the way, texted mom I love you
Closed my eyes hoping it all wasn't true
Classroom door opened, and there he stood
His face so blank, wondering how he could
He was that kid, always quiet and alone
So many guns, just shooting everyone
Here I lay and it seems so cruel
That this would be...my last day of school

Lawrence Bergman
Abington, MA

Loving My Adopted Child

I loved her in that breathless gasp

of the old mother who felt the stir
She was the child who changed
The crone to champion
No madonna, for one fist held
The sword as one hand
Held her own
I could have killed what would
Cause her tears

Now we have aged,
Her to beauty marked by
What I never was
And me by years bringing
What I could not
We feed the birds and share our words
In ordinary ways
She does not know that covered deep
Is the glitter of my blade

Jody Serey
Glendale, AZ

To Critics Who Shame Trauma Survivors Who Use Poetry as a Means to Cope

i'm sorry that i was raped
i'm not sorry that you are uncomfortable that i was raped
i'm not sorry that me getting raped makes you so uncomfortable that your
body suddenly can't move like mine couldn't
i still cry about it
i still flinch when my body inches further inside itself when i'm hugged too
long
i'm sorry that sometimes hugs hold me hostage
even though they're such an innocent thing to consent to
did he hear what i didn't consent to?
am i allowed to feel comfortable in a body that, on some occasions, was
not mine?
how i still prefer to keep the lights on in times of intimacy, because if
there's a light on, there's a way out
or how a lovers hands dance across my neck with the intent to pull me
closer
in the way that lust filled finger tips do
and i tense for fear of not having permission to scream
i'm sorry that me getting raped affects how i receive affection
sometimes i forget that it even happened
i'm not sorry that this is yet another rape poem
a triumph amongst tragedy, a war raging in the chest of every boy and girl
that had their body rampaged
we will write about it, we will bare scars and share trauma

Anai Evans
New York, NY

How?

I don't know how much longer I can hold on.
They say to be strong.
They say I will get through this.
They say that they love me.
They say to hold on.
But I can't.
It's getting harder and harder everyday.
How can I go on?
Nothing can help me.

Mackenzie Goodman
Georgetown, IN

My Son

God brought me an angel, the apple of my eye,
sent to me from heaven above, with twinkles in his eyes.
I asked God to bring you, I asked him every day,.
I never gave up hope, I just continue to pray.
It took God some time indeed to find the right one,
but He blessed me with the perfect son.
I am here to watch over you, to help you along your way.
To show you what's right from wrong, and to love you every day.
I'm here to help you grow into lend a helping hand,
to show you how to love and how to be a man.
God was really happy when He saw what He had done,
for blessing a mother with her first-born son.

Jodie Brantley
East Jordan, MI

The Twilight Hours Belong to Lovers

the stars dance tonight, you murmur, head laying on my shoulder
i look up, your hair tickling my ear as i do, vision fogged by our condensing
breath, lights shimmering in the haze, alluding to a song my hands press
against the rough, cool concrete, my body rising in turn, joint by joint as
a thought takes shape you take my hand, unfolding upwards until we are
both standing, swaying to a chorus of crickets the night is no longer so
heavy, we lift, from heels to the balls of our feet, to our toes and then their
tips, until a ballerina's pose is granted ascension love is held not to gravity's
bounds, and the laws of physics were never so easily broken by a kiss
fireflies rise with us, as if they too can hear the song, guiding us upwards
as we tango above the grass, above the trees, above the clouds, until we
are so close that we can see the stars for what they truly are lovers, like us,
that part so we can join their constellating samba romeo and juliet pass
by our left, twirling, gatsby and daisy traipse above us, half a century and
decades away is another pair, strange, and yet, familiar they smile with
our mouths, and their love is so impossibly like ours that we can feel it
from light years away they are the us that never went back down, who
never returned to earth your eyes match mine, and we begin to dance
downwards, descending some great and invisible staircase knowing even
as we do, that we would not dance like this again for nothing in heaven is
imperfect, and it is our imperfections that we cherish most in each other
my feet touch down onto dew wet grass, then yours, and the sky is still as
it has been every other day in our lives as it will be for the rest of our lives
but someday, when our hearts are also still, the sky will sway once again,
and they will play our song as dawn breaks

Jocelyn Spear
Floresville, TX

Trust Him!

Life is Impossible,
Until,
We let GOD Lead...
Then the path opens up,
And the way becomes Bright!

Jill Rene Manning
Sahuarita, AZ

Missing You

The daily struggles
Have become less painful.
I still miss you,
But I know you want me to remain strong.
It feels near impossible
On certain days,
But your voice echoes in my mind,
Telling me to have faith
For we will meet again.
Your place now is with the Lord,
Who loves us all as much as you loved me and more.
I'll keep you close to my heart,
Because my love will never falter,
And I know that one day we will meet again.

John Keith Kohles
Mason City, IA

A Harvest of Clichés

My train has left the station. My ship has left the port.
My flight has left the tarmac. Could my time be running short?
My rocket left the launchpad and I was not aboard.
I rolled the dice and bought the farm, but never drew my sword.
When Elvis left the building, I found his written note.
My timing was impeccable, it said, "that's all she wrote!"
I broke a leg while strutting, my stuff upon the stage.
And backed into a corner, I refused to act my age.
When looks and brains were handed out, I was behind the door.
My clock was running late again, when told to mind the store.
But I got a grip and held my tongue and drew my own conclusions.
I wracked my brain for peace of mind, but suffered from delusions.
It was pedal to the metal, at the old college try.
But I was whistling past the graveyard, while eating humble pie.
While looking for my pot of Gold, I was lost in outer space.
I always knew my address, but I never knew my place.
I know I wore my welcome out, when I stayed at the fair.
Both biding time and trucking on, I never had a care.
I've cooked my goose so many times, I know I should have learned -
that when you play with fire, your bridges can get burned.
A four-leaf clover I looked over, while lying in the grass.
Did I try to curry favor, when I polished up the Brass?
I'm not sure what my problem is, but I enjoy the pause
when I stop to smell the roses, and savor the applause.
I can't recapture memories, that I forgot to make.
So life's a beach, and waiter, I'll just have a piece of cake!

James Michael Fulcomer
Lincoln, CA

Lil Dixie Lilly

Lil Dixie want'cha come out and play,
Come out an play?!
Boy I gotta work all day.
All day you gotta work you say?
All day that's what I say,
I gotta pluck them weeds afta i peel these peas,
Then on my knees i gotta milk that cow,
Ya can't do that later?
Nah, I gotta do that now.
Why Now?
Momma say it's milk ah turn sour,
Dixie Lilly I'll come back in ah few hours,
Ah few hours?
By then I'll be out back helping momma plant ah few flowers,
Dixie you ain't got no time to play so i best be on my way,
Didn't i say I'll be working all day?!
Dixie, ya seen talking to that lil nappy headed boy from across the way,
So just what you and him had to say?
Nothing momma he just asked if I could come out and
Play?!! Child it ain't no time to play. He can help feed them horses over
there that bale of hay!
Then I told him Momma I got to work all day and I ain't got no time to
play!

Monica H. Thomas
Gainesville, FL

The People You Love

Sometimes when the people you love
Don't care anymore...
You have to become silent,
Because if your love didn't work,
Why would your words...
I've slowly become quiet
They don't notice.
I'm not far from them
The ones who abandoned me
Chasing the love of these humans
They made me feel wanted
Now, when I crawl into corners
They look away
And laugh.
No one cares anymore...
Not in real life.

Kai Rocke
Mendota Heights, MN

A Love of Lament

Savor the pain that covered you with gestures of malice
The tempest devouring you for it's everlasting pleasure
Give permission for submission to darkness
Not because you are weakened
But that you are not a slave to your boundaries
Narrow sight summoning a shallow essence that stalks
Every microscopic manner with the ethic of a scholar
The prejudice against the fate of drawing blood remain
Then limbs begin to fail as the foundation become prey
Forced to your knees as your ability to stand decays
Understand that ignorance will be premature revelation

Don Johnson
Detroit, MI

Love Lifted Me

Love lifted me during my storm.
God's love lifted me when I could no longer press on.
As I traveled through the valley and press through the vehement rain.
God's love lifted me above every altitude of pain.
As I sat silently awake at night but somewhat raging aloud.
God's love lifted me as though I were a little child.
Love lifted me.

Natashia Johnson
Lakeland, FL

Angels

My Doctors are great angels,
with such soft gentle eyes,
and great minds
I lay entranced upon my bed,
'Is this like when one dies?',
 my mind sinks into the green ocean,
how was it he was here?
why was he hovering, I was inclined,
to ask, but I in pain
Did not have strength to move or watch,
I seemed completely in dream,
there was no way that I could speak
An answer, I felt too numb.
He spread his wings and flew away,
the mists rolled in above,
and I sensed that I just had to pray,
"A Di Da Phat" I said
My heart was filled with love like the red tulip.
I raised my head and looked around,
and then suddenly I knew
It was a dream and with awareness, saw
my angels had been my doctors!

Natasa Cuc To
Gainesville, VA

A Dog's Wish

I wish I have a place to lay my head
Nothing big or soft just a blanket for a bed.
A place to sleep without being afraid
I had one once but I was betrayed.
They said I was bad and did something wrong,
So in their house I do not belong.
Outside I went and on a chain,
Hot, cold, snow and rain.
No shelter and not much food or water,
Scraps snuck to me by my owner's daughter.
I wish I had a place where I could fill my belly,
I wouldn't even care if it was a little smelly.
I am getting old and a little sick,
My fur is ratted with fleas and ticks.
No one will save a dog that looks like this
But every day I wish and wish.
I hear a voice I do not know,
My chain is gone and they say it's time to go.
Can it be.. Did my wish come true?
Warmth, food and water, and the words I love you.
I have a place to lay my head,
And yes it is a big soft bed.
Food in my belly and no longer sick,
In my fur no longer fleas and ticks.
My wish came true every one of them,
I even have a collar with a little gem.
I am older now and my time is near,
And that is ok, because this has been my best year.

Nancy Stoy
Washougal, WA

Time Runs Short

No I'm not ok
Knowing there's nowhere else to stay
It's not alright
Not knowing where I'm gonna lay my head at night
The deadline draws closer
And this with all the potentials I can't hope for
It's either too much or I'm not a good fit
And now it's too late for me to feel excitement
Cause I tried and I failed
All my hopes are impaled
And now I'm in a position
where I won't have a kitchen
And if I'm out in the streets
I don't know who I'll meet
So I'll pray and I'll cry
And hope to stay alive
To find an ad that isn't fake
Lord please cut me a break
So I can find roof for head
And lay in my bed
Not that long till the hammer falls
And it's the last time I roam these halls
And all I remember is that I tried and I failed

Nic Amaro
San Diego, CA

Naughty in the Grotto

Two little boys in the grotto being naughty
Having a very unique party
Attendance in class was very tardy
Caught by Sister with a seed
Misty air was what she sneezed
Thought you missed her smoking that weed
To the office she took you boys
Time for class not funny-smelling toys
Don't seem sad, but very overjoyed
Stop smoking around your school
What you're doing is against the rules
Now you're in trouble with lots of fools
Storing it in the St. Mary statue
Was an idiotic thing to do
Now everyone's laughing at you
Places you go you want to fight
Things you do are just not right
Remember, what you do in the dark shines in the light
Maybe before the age of forty
You'll engage in a different kind of party
So you can stop acting so naughty

Maria Clavo
New Orleans, LA

Winter Sunrise

Upturned face, eyes wide open, satisfied smile.
Basking in the pink light of morning.
The sun rises to greet the day.
Crisp air hangs silent as the snow settles,
Sparkling in the dawn.

Karin Mahoney
Point Pleasant Boro, NJ

Alone at Christmas

Oh bless me lord this christmas so I wont be all alone,
Bring a joy and a spirit to my house so it will feel like its a home.
I know 'Ive done some wrong things in these long and lonely years,
But I promise ill do better if you'll help me dry these tears.
Oh Lord I need your glory, I need your shining light,
To brighten up my path so I can keep you in my sights.
Im down here on my knees giving my life back to you,
Oh Lord please help me, im tired of being sad and blue.
I need to be filled up, to be like an angel from above,
Then I can spend this holiday spreading goodness and love.
Oh Lord ill work with your help to make this all come true,
And finally maybe spend this christmas with a few more people than just
me and you....

Corey Welch
Boonville, MO

Little Beast

Little beast,
Your tooth and nail clattering against the metal heat.
The quiet rings, yet deafens, echoes.
You whine like a frightened deer.
The red leers from the corners of your eyes.
You don't know about lies.
You only know your open-book face.
You only know how to pace out your fear like a lion.
You wield your wild like a sword.
You wield your inner child like an axe.
Shiver and shake.
You're slowly sinking in a lake like a drowning rat.
Shiver and shake.
You climb out and heave for air, rake in the land under your feet.
Twitch.
Are you finally still? Where is your will?
Fight. Scratch. Claw.
There is no law in this land of my heart, only the wind.
However, even the wind must be tamed.
I will not be shamed because of you.
You are but small,
Only a little beast.

Morgen Mariah Chambers
Elizabethtown, KY

7 Misguided Bullets

Life is too short and death comes to early for some
He was...is...now
Removed
7 misguided bullets from front and from back
Dead leaves on the ground
And minds are left wondering
And hearts fall apart
Like quicksand sinks into a puzzle of questions and fire
breathing accusations and people asking why
But questions go unanswered
And whys are undiscovered
Because diamonds are in a class of their own and we aren't worthy
Of a talent so strong, and a brain so big, and a kind spirit who shouldn't
have gone out like he did
So we send cards and flowers full of empty words, because
death is often misunderstood
His body is gone, but his spirit remains, and I keep asking questions
and holding back tears and looking at pictures and re-watching vids
Just to hear his voice and to see his face
Because my mind can't convince my heart that he's gone

Elizabeth J. Campbell
Sherman Oaks, CA

Want What You Are

You are my strength when I feel like I'm weak.
I want to speak the every word that you think is sweet.
You are the beauty when I feel like the beast.
I want to be your protection when there are no police.
You are my smile when my face simply can't.
I want to be the hand that you reach for when it's time for that dance.
You are the biggest promotion that I strive for
that I try for so hard to advance.
I want to be the person of interest when and if there's ever that chance.
You are my success when I feel like I've failed.
I want to be the person who was with you in any story you tell.
You are the only pretty face I want to see once I gently lift up that vail.
I want to be the love letter that you wait for everyday in the mail.
You are the path I've always prayed for when opportunity shows.
I want to be the light that you depend on when you need it to glow.
You are the only one I want to be telling when no one else knows.
I want to be the guidance that you follow when you feel there's no other
place you can go.

Mark Turner
Monroeville, PA

Walking Through Life

I'm walking
To a place
Where honesty is upheld above all
Where journalists value accuracy and credibility
Where they are motivated by their responsibility to accurately inform the
public
And not to just receive a paycheck
Because honesty should be valued above money
I'm walking
To a small house by the sea
To a man that loves, treasures, and values me
A man who challenges me to fulfill my dreams
And as he plays with our children
I rub my wedding ring knowing that I made the right choice
I am walking every day
Towards my dreams, hopes, and goals
But being on this walk has made me question everything I know
I have messed up, made mistakes, failed a few times, and been hurt in the
deepest way possible
But still I walk
Walk towards my future career as an honest journalist
Walk towards my life as a mother and wife
Walk towards the best part of me
Yes, I am scared
Yes, I am afraid to fail and not achieve everything I want for my life
But as long as I have this persistence and determination in my heart
Then I will keep on walking towards my future

Moriah Ayana Mason
Hoover, AL

What Does It Take?

Sometimes moving forward means having the courage to stay still
harden your will with memories.
Trust me it won't take eternity
envision the person you want to be.
What will you do for others instead of yourself?
People who was there from the start
they are the ones true to your heart.
Treat your loved ones like precious fruit
healthy and sweet continue to grow together.
What does it take... Courage.
Avoid building your dreams with sand
waves of change will wash them away.
There is no shame in biding your time.
You wanna transform?
Become a butterfly without the cocoon?
better luck next time when there's a blue moon.
What does it take... Dreams.
Show appreciation for what you have before wanting more.
Trust me, what you want can't be bought in stores
promises from strangers are like Toys R Us
empty, out of business, with nothing to discuss.
New friends come with a golden touch
fake smiles while they use you as a crutch
giving you in return, excuse after excuse to compensate.
Now, you ask what it takes
all you had to do was appreciate.

Noel Torres
Bronx, NY

What Are You Thinking?

What are you thinking?
A question I have always had about you.
What goes through that lovely mind of yours?
Not even your body language can help.
Do you think about me?
Do you think about what we could be?
Do you love me as much as you say you do?
Or do you love someone else too?
What are you thinking when we kiss?
Are you in a state of bliss?
What are you thinking when I say "I love you"?
I hope it's "I love you too."
All this uncertainty in my head
Makes me feel like our love is dead.
My heart is endlessly sinking
So please tell me, what are you thinking?

Camilo Patino
Elizabeth, NJ

Something Worse Than the Dark

I've known what it's like to fear my own mind,
Beheld the terror behind a smile.
I've heard the echo, hollow and frank,
While into the gloom, I sank.

I am in darkness,
So darkness, I become –
Whilst wandering forests black and deep,
Lost, in Eternal sleep.

I've met the monsters and ghosts alike,
That thrive within my soul.
They always win,
And so, I never lose –
Yes, I am in full control.

I desire those things
That destroy in the end,
A ship on a stormy sea.

I feared the dark before I learned -
That the dark is afraid of me.

Pallas-Amenah TeNette Wright Morgan
Silver Spring, MD

Dance with His Demons

Words tumble from your mouth of all the things I don't know about you
I see the demons you try to hide from me
I see your good and your bad and sit in stunned silence
The strong quiet type, the hero who believes he's the villain
You see me as good, some kind of innocent, but there are things you don't
know about me
You don't know that I long to dance with your demons, I want to be the
one who quiets them
When your mind is racing I want be the break that stops it
When your storm is taking over I want to be your sun
All that bad that you see only makes me love you more
While others may have run from you I want nothing more then to run to
you
I want to wrap you in my arms and wash away every bad memory and
every sad thought
I wish to see all of you and to know every secret
So tonight my love let me dance with your demons

Paige Elizabeth Jackson
Portland, OR

Vessel of Aphrodite

Within the bowels of the monsoon
Carried high to the stars
 To only drown in acidic drops upon my flesh
Arms reach thy hips
Fingers are constantly reminded
To have been made to thrum the white & black shells to a siren's voice
Instead they have chosen to spell words upon the sand
Only to disappear when the sea has read them
Skin melanin
Never once has yearned to be cleansed by an oysters pearl
To reflect the skin of Aphrodite
The sun has never seared thy tone to burn red
Eyes of thy earth to what holds the sea from sinking
Does not want to be washed to have eyes of Aphrodite
Jawline can etch a scar upon another's eyes
Aphrodite does not like
Brown sugar blows with the wind,
5 years following thy monsoon the sugar passes thy hips
Braids entwined with leaves of autumn can be formed
Up high, gripped by the vines of the jungle where my ancestors roam
You'd think thy hand grips the ends of brown sugar to sear it from my scalp

Nia Ariana Manivanh
Yelm, WA

My Son

I tapped my heart
It tapped back twice
They placed you in my arms
It tapped back thrice
I have never stared so deep into a soul
Of gray green eyes
Missing you like I have never missed another
Even as I held you close
I felt you
Leave

Lori I. Cain
Salem, OR

The Dark

The dark can be your friend yet an enemy
At night you can stare at the ceiling and not worry about anything
it's like the world stops for a few hours and you're free
but some nights when the dark becomes the enemy you lay awake
thinking something bad is going to happen
and suddenly all your fears come to your mind and it's a battle to go to
sleep
each night brings a new mystery

Nerissa Christina Tidmore
Norfolk, VA

Barter, Won't You?

Take this rose,
Beware not of any thorn
Any blood shed will be quelled
By my knotted tongue;

Take this trumpet,
Hesitate not of any tremble
Any surge felt will be stomped
By my heavy heart;

Take this stone
Refrain not of any pound
Any balance seized will be caught
By my ready hand;

Take my leaf
Quiver not of any words
All fear bent will be stolen
By my haunted mind;

From all taken, lend me an
Eye.

Oyéb Photte
Los Angeles, CA

Who Could Ask for Anything Better?

My mouth opens in a frozen gawp.
Sauce, dribbles down chin.
My eyes, attracted to.
Glib glistenings of.
Caught with the sauce, shimmering,
bits of runneled cheese, still shiny.
American cheddar retention.
Evocative views; plastic encased mercenary.
Thumbs. Numbs.
Screen lies blank, or did I?
Parceling out the divisions.
Next intentions.
Spitooned versions of burger tumble out.
Realms of new economics, splattered through trade wars.
Green New Deals intersect in bowels of coal mined earth; fracks.
Take our cattle, but don't let us grind.
Emoluments of manure swags.
Methane rolls in sheets of fog.
Take those lands when least expected, I can, can't I?
Wall provided by the other adjoining Country.
Burger unhinges from channeled fist.
Feelings of Volleyball expanding in chest.
Infections of air to carry down in robed neglegance.
Fated burger box crinkles as arms drop.
Volleyball explodes...

John V. Mallahan
Bellingham, WA

Nothing

Nothing is what you made me believe I was
 Nothing is what you treat me as
Nothing is what you see me as
Nothing is what I say I am
Nothing is what I feel after you broke me
Nothing is what I say when you ask me what's wrong
Nothing is what people know
Nothing is something
Something is the flowers you bring me
Something is the flutter in my chest
Something is the smile on my face
Something is the smell of your cologne
Something is the way you look at me
Something is the warmth of your embrace
Something is the love I feel when I'm with you
Something is the time we spend together
Something is the way I feel when I'm not with you
Something is the thing I will promise you

Madicen Grace Prince
Nesbit, MS

Within His Eyes

Serendipity I've felt.
You've been making my soul melt.
Again the worlds disappear,
Just you and I on this dirt sphere.
I've discovered two emeralds.
Thoughts flee, sanity unfolds.
I dream of the green allure,
A sight I'll endlessly savor.
Deep in those two precious stones,
Are questions asked in whispered tones.
Soundless to the physical ear,
But piercing in what spirits hear.
The window into the soul
Is where one finds life's loophole.
We discover what was meant
Before beyond was bent.
This moment reveals a glance
Of a concept captured by chance.
Substance between entities,
Sensed over seen identities.

Marissa Leigh Camp
Beaver, PA

Don't Forget I Love You

If I yell at you,
If tell you to leave me alone,
If I run away from my problems,
If I lose my way,
Don't forget I Love You.
If I died tomorrow,
If my soul left this earth,
Whether it was self inflicted,
Or if someone took away my right to live,
Or if God just needed me,
Don't forget I Love You.
You may forget the smell of my hair,
You may forget the sound of my voice,
You may forget the feeling of my hugs and kisses,
But don't forget I Love You.

Kimberly Lovalvo
New castle, IN

Today's Black Child

Black Child, Black Child do not blame yourself, integration is the reason you've gone and lost your wealth.
It started with the Moors when they traveled overseas and enabled the Europeans to change your history.
Even during Jim Crow your family was living well, but they sold their soul to America, so now You live in hell.
Then came babies having babies, and that's where you come in - never received the rich tradition your parents were supposed to send.
Now you're being shot in the back and incarcerated for no reason, OH! I understand quite well why you have your thoughts of treason.
Society is to blame tho, fore they put you in this place - a place of total chaos with a stain upon your race.
But your present will be your past soon so you know what you must do, remove that stain from upon your face and reveal the purity in You.
It's unfortunate all you've been through, this country has treated you foul - so I offer my sincere apology, to you, Today's Black Child.

Michael Hare
Newport News, VA

The Navy Veteran

The old man sat at the kitchen table
with his granddaughter and grandson.
His eyes glistened, he hoisted his hands
and launched his life story for the tenth time
that year. The old man glanced from
the girl to the boy, back and forth, a rhythm
of oars paddling to the shore.
The boy grew weary and began closing
his eyes while the old man turned toward
the girl. She fought not to laugh when
her sleeping brother awoke to attention.
The old man trudged onward,
reporting his significant stories with passion.
The old man ended, recalling a horizon-
A story the girl had never heard
A story the boy slept during
But the last story she learned before
The patriot journeyed home.

Morgan Carlock Clark
Kansas City, MO

The Trapped Escapee

She has forgotten a decade of her life,
Oblivious to most of the torment they've endured.
Her siblings would call her lucky,
Jealous of her "ability" to become an escapee,
But there are two sides to every story.
She's terrified and a little more at risk,
To fall into similar patterns for life lessons she did miss.
She's terrified because she keeps forgetting,
Key moments most cannot stop remembering.
She has an obsession with the clock,
Because she's trying to keep track,
Of the time she hasn't blacked out.
She'll count the hours, minutes, seconds,
But before she knows it, she's out.
She'll realize much later that half the day has passed.
Her memory of it all, however, is not intact.
She's free from all tragedies,
But she'd give that up to remember other things.

Jack Hall
Mohawk, NY

When We Share

Our love will not falter,
we bring change in together.
In truth we can claim,
a new world free of terror.
The earth can be shared,
and the surface repaired.
We have a great power,
and it will come when we share.

Matt Buonocore
Manlius, NY

Observing the Deserving

The Market Teeming with Diverse People
Gazing at Every Human Form
Listening to Snippets of Conversation
Judging Not, But Questioning Their Norm
As All March in Trances of a Divergent Dream
Each Embracing Their Own Worldly Steeple
While Children Play Before Being Coerced to Conform
Asking Who is Knowing, What is Known and How it will Seem
As the Masses Gather from Divided Directions to Perform
Alienating Actions Devoid of Listening with Singular Reclamation
Seeing More, Knowing Less, Wondering
Is Eternal Searching All We Deserve?

Raymond Murray
New City, NY

Unconditional

Love is not blind
Insane at times
You touch my heart
I'm blessed, yes.
For you are mine, till infinite time.

Nagella Jean-Baptiste
Brooklyn, NY

Blue Eyes

Oh how you make me smile.
How you make me sweat when you get close and I can feel the trickle of hair
from your forearm.
Light goosebumps underneath my fingers as I glide them down your spine.
My body shivers as your warm delicate breath caresses my neck in a familiar
way.
Sync as our bodies collide in a rhythm of passion.
Smooth as hands slither down my torso and settle with my thigh.
An explosion of warmth consumes my soul as a calm comfort overtakes me.
I awake to see such beauty and love and there in the moment are your blue eyes!

Ashley Stevens
Columbia Station, OH

Power Through Pain

In anticipation
for amnesia
to unfold.
The scars
on your heart,
are covered
by the lies
you believe.
For protecting it is vital,
or , so you think.
For there is
power through pain,
and a time to heal.

Lisa Loraine Henderson
Conover, NC

Tryst of Dedication

The lotus blooms upon the ebon pond.
Ivory moon beset upon a jet sky.
The scars of battle a sanguine stain on alabaster sands.
A tear drop falls upon the infernal plane.
Worlds collide upon a kiss.
Her eyes glisten in the passion as his darken in the abyss.
Heavens fall and the hells rise.
Together as one they breathe, fate undaunting in their hands.

Daniel S. Small
Startup, WA

Close Call

From each last brush of pain and blood
drips off my chest as pouring rain.
As time no longer exists,
longing to make it to the other side of this,
With the professional gazers surrounded me about,
with looks of hope but so much more of doubt,
in my mind racing, my body yet still,
in my chest paceing,
thinking was this the very last time,
I'd meet the eyes of ones loved,
as they are emersed from crying,
Inside slowly dying,
but for everyone among me I'm saving face,
timely fighting,
on my own behalf,
while making the moments significant
and to last,
Admireing the idea there's still hope in a chance,
The chambers of life trying to close,
they say it's to soon to call what the outcome will bring,
no one yet knows,
As they put me in a calm state,
I'm off to sleep,
hours later,
I awake and me my fate,
To still be here among my family,
loved ones and bloodline,
and im grateful though in agonizing pain,
but no grasp of time,
My words now hold so true to everyone I meet or know,
never take a mere second for granted,
it's to close to call,
if we stay and when we might Go.

Mary E. Holt
Milton, WI

Creations on a Whim

You were created on a memory of something I thought would last a
lifetime...

But that was not in the cards..
And neither were you..

now I'm left to mourn you on the once vibrant banks of a sea named
Liquid Poetry.

It seems I am the only soul that cared about your too early demise..
I'm the only one who seems to care enough to visit your memory..
To help you remain as real and tangible as you were.
Even though it was a lifetime ago...

You were created in the comfort of a memory I thought would last a
lifetime...

You perished in the womb of a shattered spirit..
I know now you died from the result of a broken heart..
And I am so sorry.

You were created from a memory I thought would last a lifetime.
You will be remembered with a love that will span infinite eternities.

Maryah Langston
Ocklawaha, FL

I Woke Up This Morning

I woke up this morning
whether it's raining or pouring
above the storm clouds
the eagles are soaring
looking to the heavens above
waiting and watching for hummingbirds and doves
and each and every day
if we get to say:
"I woke up this morning,"
we have a purpose to serve
with grace and mercy we may not deserve
but it is a gift from above
flight from a descending dove
we may be tired at times
with or without reasons or rhymes
but trudge on my friend
even when you cannot see the end
because you woke up this morning

Mark Daniel Schnell
Louisville, KY

Heartbroken

The year 2019 began like any other
With nothing to write home to mother
As the month rolled on by
Things were not so fine
I had to say farewell
To a friend I called sunshine
A few months went on by
And my heart sank again
I had to say good-bye to a lady
Who was my sister and best friend
We grew up together side by side
Now she's not here to go for a ride
Shortly after losing my sister
My heart was broken in two
I lost the love of my life
The best husband I ever knew
We were together 34 years
I've never shed so many tears
With my loved ones gone so peaceful
Life will be different for a while
They were always there to listen
And could brighten my day with a smile

Mary Ann Hollander
Walters, OK

Begin Again

If this is the end of everything
Everything will begin again
Dead ends are only new beginnings in disguise
We just don't know what they look like
Hope belongs in the darkest places
Hope belongs on our faces
If this is the end of everything
Everything will begin again
These days people don't text back
Or have a sense of tact
I wish you would say something
Something is better than nothing
If this is the end of everything
Everything will begin again
The world is a cruel place
Don't let it mess up your beautiful face
They say money corrodes and corrupts
Hey look America I see a lot of rust
If this is the end of everything
Everything will begin again

Jeremy Skidmore
Springfield, MI

Back to the World

This endless year
It's become quite clear
I'll never return
Will just continue to burn
It's all a joke
A living bad stroke
And no matter how I try
Or how much I cry
"Back to the world" I can't come
My total sum
The me, I am
Stuck in Viet Nam

Poet Rasheed
Little Rock, AR

A Life That Follows

Silent whispers of shadows play;
Shadows of whispers silent, stay;

Silent play of shadowed whispers, walk;
Stay of whispered shadows silent, talk;

Silent whispers of shadows sneak;
Shadows of whispers silent, creak;

Silent sneak of shadowed whispers, sing;
Creak of whispered shadows silent, bring!

Jeremiah Patrick Rose
Ligonier, PA

Cries of a Homeless Child

Through mists of morning light the homeless child
begins her day, wondering where her life will go.
In the endless lines waiting for a hot meal to ease
hungers ache. Her mother alone is her refuge and safety.
Oh, the cries of a homeless child, searching for a place
to lay her head in peace.
Oh, the cries of a homeless child, still praying to God
for a home.
The darkness comes again, the homeless child and mother,
sleep in cardboard boxes as shields from the wind.
The mother watches over her child to see that no harm befalls her child,
getting
very little sleep. This is the life of a homeless child.
Oh, the cries of a homeless child, slowly losing hope.
Oh , the cries of a homeless child, slowly dying in despair.
This is the life of a homeless child.

Youlanda Marie Thompson
Tupelo, MS

The Desire of Something Dangerous

The desire of something dangerous
Is dangerous within itself
They say the longing of something dangerous
Is not beneficial for my health
I want to jump off of rooftops
To see if I can fly
They say I cannot do this
For if I did, I would surely die
I want to stand out in the rain
As lightning pierces the sky
They say I cannot do this
For if I did, I would surely die
I want to sink to the ocean's bottom
And study fish from where I lie
They say I cannot do this
For if I did, I would surely die
But when I try to ask them
The reason as to why
They say they cannot tell me
For that information they can't supply

Kaitlyn Elizabeth Jones
Suffolk, VA

Voices of Fugue

Mourning is lost when all becomes a tragedy.
Numbness the cost, and grief loses all meaning
Coalesce unfulfilled, exhaustion, apathy
virtue not as dead as damned to only dreaming.

At salvation's out thrust hand, smear mistrust and damning
for atonement is at once both horrible and cleansing.

A flag cannot recall a day at full mast
hanging at half so long
Disaster, a stronger word in the past
and weeping knew where to belong.

Division smoldering smothers solidarity
derision's cloud births a smoke banshie
Strength gives way to weakness of the soul
as diamond wisdom reverting back to coal.

Echoes each day's unending funeral dirge,
fugues to quell, not only the fire, but the urge.

Are we to find life now so contemptuous
as to only seek disambiguation of death?
The very image of once empyrean spirits, callus
reduced to recounting each ragged breath.

Scot Dunlap
Clinton, TN

Dearest Dad

My Dearest Dad,
My heart is aching from the hurt you are going through that brings you much pain that you do not deserve. The memories appear in my of our past that we shared of joys and sorrows, where you were my anchor in saying no matter what comes there is a tomorrow: when you believe in the life beautiful, and you held me in your loving arms. I look back over the years to see the great strengths you shown from your great skill to make things of beauty that moves those around you by what created from you dear caring hands. Dad, you always made time for me in what I needed and shared your knowledge of life that I hold dearly in my heart, my beating heart that I share with those who needs help. My heart aches in the hurt you endured in our life, where you never complain or shed a tear except the day your dear love, Mom was called to God. Which hurts me so much seeing you with so much sadness like I am feeling right now when you called to our Lord Savior Jesus Christ. But I know you can once again be with your beautiful love, my Mom and can be happy. As this all, I ever wanted to you and our family who I love dearly in my heart! I hope you know how much I love you and can be proud of me in what I do for our family that means so much to me. I keep seeing little things that remind me of you and know though you are not here with us now that you are not far because I carry your love deep in my heart! I know time will ease my painful loss though I want to let you know I will never forget you and will never let your memory fade away! Dad please know you always loved by our family and me and you will never be forgotten because as long as we live you will live: as we are your legacy that will hold dearly in our hearts that loves you so much! Take care my dearest Dad and from time to time come by to say hello as we welcome you always and we continue living. Though it will be rough at times, we can make because you were our teacher and Dad who taught us well who we will love always!

Love your son,

Robert Louis Nacke
Colfax, WI

I Miss You . . .

Why did you have to go so far?
Couldn't you have seen that which was near
sustaining us with the richness of your life
instead of leaving us with a hollowness that
grips our entire body leaving it halved—
like the shell after the meat of the nut has been eaten—
Empty
What was it you wanted?
Did you have to ask the question instead of accepting
the answers all around you, drawing on them
to fulfill your unquenchable need to know—
staying awhile to sip and savor the drink at hand
instead of gulping down the nectar, leaving the glass—
Empty
What did you find?
Was it all you had hoped for, was it worth the sacrifice
or did you suddenly realize that the want was in
the search and the search did not reward your curiosity,
looking and finding nothing to warrant the fact that you are—
Gone.

Carmie Mason
Bellmawr, NJ

Sacrosanct Conception

The chartreuse green of the bud in the spring,
the way the wind makes the bell chimes ring,
are sounding sacrosanct conception. Elaborate, in
the same direction the glass of rubied wine tells of
the fullness from the Creator of time. Velveteen
violets soaking in the warmth of the evening sun.
Firm, fragrant fragile too somewhat like you. Every
morn royal, purposed, few.
The secret known of what's gone and to come will always
be align with the Holy
One. Not by force all things with love is the resounding
answer from above. And with all the wisdom of what
rings true, these are the gifts God has given to me, and
to you. Kingdom come, high hopes for you. As sunlight
shines through sparkle dew, aspiration, I've prayed
you'd knew, the Savior, tried and true. Wrapped in
magenta imperial purple hue wanting for holy touch to
know you to love so much. Affinity, ostrich egg rarity a
psalm a parody joy filled hilarity absolute no vanity.
Highborn empyrean, regal, pompous pretty, onlookers
take pity. A consecration consumed, Utopian enrollment.
Atonement, enrobing putting on of the new man
promised land potent. Blessedness, pearly gates
happiness awaits. Afterworld wonderful, the sky full of
electric thunder. Enamored in your ways Ancient of
Days, never go away. Keep me close as to not stray.

Joan Dutkin
Sarasota, FL

Debbie Inspired

No diamond in the rough
This woman so exquisitely cut
Set within a heart of gold
One that tarnish will never dull
A beauty so very desired
One that has artist inspired
So stunning an impact not seen or heard
When painted on canvas or in poetic word
The ticking hands of time seem to simple unwind
With a glimpse of her smile missed for such a long while

Michael Lee Craig
Las Vegas, NV

A Battle Never Too Big

For God, a battle is never too big.
A battle for Him is one hand up.
He can lift the world up without standing up.
I call on God for a battle like this one.
With God, I am David who won with one stone.
I can trump over a Goliath without a stumble.
With God, I am Moses with the stake in his hand.
I have power over Pharoah.
An eye for an eye was never made for me.
This battle was only made for God.

Antwanette L. Howard
Dallas, TX

The Stories We Tell

When the sun falls beneath the sea
And the stars shine brighter than a lighthouse
Could ever be

To the ocean, I must go
Where many stories are told with woe

The tales of woe that come from there
Are told from such some cannot bear

The stories we find are often bleak
And what we find is not what we seek

Many stories and tales are told
With which we feel we must keep hold

Elsa Paige Yuan Yuan Staley
Boise, ID

I Wish You Would Call

Today I woke to a beautiful day..
Took a ride thru the mountains with nothing to say..
I stopped to see the leaves softly fall..
All I could think was how I wish you would call...
There is so much I need to say...
Since you left my life has never been the same...
Tell me something Mother please...
Give me a sign or show me a clue...
I want so bad to hear you...I do..
To tell me I got this, that I will know in my heart what is true...
The only thing is I will never be able to hug you...
I know l cannot dwell on the past
But oh how I wish I could hear your words...
I would hold on to every word and I would understand at last...
Never a day goes by that my tears don't fall...
I long and wish you would call...
I hear you say you are much stronger than them all....
Go dry those eyes...
Look in to the sky's...
When you see those leaves start to fall...
Then you will know that is my way of giving you a call....

Timmi Jimette Mann
Ozark, AR

Looking Out the Window Through Bare Feet

Ten past six and the stars had taken refuge.

I found myself in wait for the black bird
(the red feathered, red tipped beaked one
that met me there on occasions in search of
wheat bread crumbs and sunflower seeds)
to find its way to rest outside my window.

The summer wasn't virgin anymore;
the way its sun caressed and tongued my naked feet
made it evident.

The sky was quilted with what looked like
powdered orangish-grays in its horizon,
like that picture I once saw in Jack London Square
a hundred and twenty-three months ago.

"Sorry friend but I have nothing for you today!"

It read my mind,
then smiled and flew off into the morning.

William Morris Thurston III
Sacramento, CA

Paint a Picture Black and Gray

Pull out the easel, set the canvas positioned long slender clean slate.
Sketch the figures huddled dark bound hostage as innocence abates
   to charcoal cooled coals etching burned bronzed images;
Faceless entities slipping in and out the background crying
   earth toned sojourners accepting, numbered, alone, quiet, dying;
Still the images in silence, hard, disfigured, grotesque horrors in place,
apart;
Somber soul drained eyes skeletal, socket holes, frail boned, buried in the
heart;
Let tears fall down their cheeks in wonder, awe, fear of what happens next.
Acrylic primers dilute the trembling wash in a historic story line vexed
   flaking and cracking each soul, truth in polyptych blended burnish
bleeds
Hushed, quiet, soft exuding whimpered cries, chiaroscuro collages of
death from life
   fading to diluent breaths of an unholy darkness and silenced strife;
Graded gouache monochrome scraper boards release sfumatos singular
communal lives
Varnish sacrificed the final rendition to camouflage the actuality of all it
denies.
Time memorialized in genocide atrocities of Native Americans,
Cambodians, Hawaiians,
   Jews, Rwandans, Armenian, Bosnia, Darfur and so many others
forgotten.
When does it stop? Is life not more precious than this?
   Until change comes, until we learn, until history is renewed with fact
Paint the Picture Black and Gray display grieve and pray then act.

D.M. Babbit
Kendall Park, NJ

Once in a Lifetime

Once in a lifetime my view meets the water like a pier as i peer into my
heart
Recognizing such a pure emotion should not appear difficult
So i take the day, the sunrise and sunset as easy as the wind blows
knowing my fingers could move those strands of hair that block your eyes

One look can speak a thousand words and set an eternity of love
I stand at the gate of your soul as nerves as child crushes
my sweet you can be my candy crush and I'll gladly get cavities for you
I will not run from you but to you because i run from deceit and to love

The sands of time glass from the burning emotion passion looks to
Our hourglass never runs out of time yet lasts forever and a day
I'll tell you i love seven time, give you seven kisses, and repeat it seven
times
I only want you to understand that we are complete so we start a new
beginning

Praying for answers brings questions and vice versa
Why should i hurt you when i know what goes around comes the same
So i continue and will continue to give you the same
knowing that in truth we find real emotion comes

Once in a life time

Albert Ashton Ellis
Round Rock, TX

Nonsense

I know the general shape of angst. Melting mint chocolate ice cream dripping down my palm. But what sets me apart are the pigeons surrounding me, a pink flamingo. As the world races by, all sports cars and hot rods I don't know the name of, as I inch by in my little blue VW bug, eating those thin extra crispy french fries. But angst isn't any of those things. It's shaped like that door that everyone leaves me through. Or the staircase I fall down every single time. It's like wanting to shove a fork in a pretty blue toaster just to watch the sparks fly. Angst is a white goose that's just a bit too loud and doesn't quite belong. Like you, goose. Just a silly old maid to Juliet or a loveless widow holding on to nothing but the money that was left to her. I'm not saying that I would decline if an old man opened his wallet to me and asked for nothing but companionship in return. Anyways, angst is shaped like the roof you sit on with friends and write songs together about your shitty lives hoping you'll never need to leave but it's a school night and your mom is out front.

Aria J. Billingsley
Loveland, CO

Ruins in Starlight

Under the fading light of a deep forgotten star.
A lost city echoes silently in the celestial dust afar.
On the shores of a saturnine ocean cold.
Black and stained with the blood of eidolons old.

Illustrious monoliths stand dead in a hollow metropoli.
Now an empery of tombstones in a desolate necropoli.
The pale spectra beauty of twin moons.
Reveals at night the spawning of antecedent doom.

Lurking within the shadows of petrified gods anonymity.
Bellows the immortelle past of the cryptic city.
And a shadow within the shadows hums a tune.
Of a long departed haply rune.

Ascending to the highest tower for a heavenly sight.
Is death eternal waiting for a cosmic show of starlight.
What appeared twinkling in dying skies.
Was an indescribable Galaxy rise.

Ignacio Jesus Velazquez
Los Angeles, CA

Truth Be

Oxytocin is my sin

You're voice under my skin,
Pressed against mine that night
You said it wasn't right

When you clenched you're mouth tight
I saw that you're eyes weren't contrite
Trying to advert you're eyesight

Scared, to start a fight

Gave me a melancholic smile
All while trying to stay in denial
A lie, you're trying to compile
Quiet, but the click of a clock dial

Those nights with white wine
A toast to forgotten times
When we felt at our prime
Still a hole in my heart; void of this rhyme

Christopher Ricks
West Haven, UT

Medi-eval Battle (Lord Byron's War)

Cursed were the bloodhounds when bark-ed they at night,
And mitered stood the sentries whose guard was palled with fright
At any sound so stealthful that might alarm them to fight.
Aye, to be wrested from encroaching battle's din,
To revel in the comfort of sheltered hearth and kin,
Freed from foul temptation to commit a murderous sin.

And breathless flakes in wondrous quiet fell upon the ground
And powdery drifts now nipped at boots and covered them with down
As if to proffer one last chance for all to dwell in calm,
Perchance to hide impending horror with nature's covering balm.

But what do men in feral march care about nature's mien?
Its magical white ambience, its whimsical, soothing ken?
And marched they on in numbing fear of what their fate had sewn
Encroaching those skittish sentries who stared into unknown.

And soon those alabaster fields ran red in crimson flow
Of life's once hallowed hopes and dreams now drowned in heartless snow,
As heaven's wintry manna that bears amorphous dreams
Lay trampled and defiled amid a thousand screams.

Lev Tov
Brooklyn, NY

Love and Peace

Love and peace, must go together
you won't find one without the other
so if you know them you will see
why these two friends will always be
love and peace, are never at war
love and peace don't stray afar
love and peace will always be
love and peace is you and me

Sharon Mohan
Deltona, FL

Celtic Crosses

Majestic Irish landscape etched in shades of green called out amidst the
rainbows radiance.
History of the lads crested throughout rolling green hills and cobble stone
streets.
Stone throw rippled across the Celtic sea, north atlantic winds call out for
the love of you and me.
Wind swept hair marched in whipped and lashed by the chill of
September's rain.
Pour me a pint of the frothy me Guinness.
Tip, tap, here comes the good ole Irish dance.
Give me a potato, give me two, one for you and one for me.
Take this blithe and starvation for we a land carved in stones of history
amidst the time honored tradition of this fair country.
Let's pour a pint and cheer to another good year!.

Jennifer Nicole Uncles
Belgrade, MT

Human

Skin and bone, nothing but flesh
But this heart beats in my chest.
I'm human, not materialistic.
Your idea of perfect is not realistic.
Flawed and scarred, broken and bruised,
I've been taken advantage of, and I've been used.
But here I stand, thriving and breathing.
I'm no longer taking the abuse I'm receiving.
I'm human in the flesh.
Take me as I am with this heart in my chest.

Macayla Bettis
Travelers Rest, SC

Love Sick

Burden by love flames
stars pour out of my heart
intuition of desire has clubbed my mind
you cannot enter into my passionate skin
transform yourself into a door
where you have no lead of despairing parts
seek to love but no boundaries will be found
but only sickness with my heart
you have no passion or drive
so keep your love while I dwell into the abyss of time

Sandra Ivette Cedres
Newark, NJ

Plastic You

Cosmetic glue of ignorance stitching up your pride
Contact with reality fell to the wayside
Imperfections covered with glossy magazines
Hiding behind staples, dollars, limousines
Foul-smelling deals filling up your schedule
Counting down the days, next knife to undergo
Scars and irritations removed with utter ease
Fill it, fix it, fake it, so desperate—aim to please
Nip and tuck, implant it, shape it to my needs
Wax and tan, relax it, cut until it bleeds
Weaving webs of lies in synthetic tufts of hair
Tangling the truth to stretch across what's bare
Breaking, bending, twisting to fit a mold they set
Bowing to the pressure of someone you never met
Blindly follow others and clone every feature well
Stop at nothing to achieve a body you can sell
Injecting fatty tissue to fill a void so thin
Burying your soul to cover pain that lies within
Statuesque in making but hollow to the touch
No person left beneath it, missing way too much
Regrets are overwhelming in a shallow hull of self
Pretty is your face, gone your mental health

Tamara L. Horton
Melrose, MN

Love Shouldn't Be Cautious

Love shouldn't be cautious.
It should be divine.
So why are people worried
when love should be fine?
Is it because of the past?
Is it because of the pain?
When it comes to love,
Theres so much more to gain.
Love shouldn't be cautious.
It should be treasured.
More valuable than good.
An endless measure.
Love shouldn't be cautious,
But I understand why.
I'll be sure to keep my heart open
And never let my love die.

Amber Louise Thornton
Searcy, AR

A Simple Tear

Here we go again another year,
With hate in our hearts and love in our tears,
Understanding this brings me closer to fear,
Why have our hearts become solid?
Is it because our hearts are broken like our wallets?
What we don't have, we seem to always miss,
And when spirits let go, our tears begin to drip,
Love is only felt through a sigh of a cry,
It's a new day an age, it's the new time,
Hearts have become broken,
People will steal a simple token,
Because material things in life have spoken,
Showing you what matters most,
You show no love to yourself or others as a host,
You feed off success, an swear that's the best,
Forgetting this is a test,
Only God will relieve your stress,
So lets try to love with justice,
Taking away your heart is a must,
Your heart is something you can't trust,
Use all your tears to love throughout the rest of the year,
And maybe everyone will hear,
The sound of love from a simple tear!

Jianna Joy Diggs
Atlantic City, NJ

Why?

Why is all i ask?
You tore my heart apart
You destroyed my self-esteem
You made me lost
You made my life go from
happy to nolonger happy
You have ruined who i used to be
Why is all I ask

Renee Edna Garcia
Goldbar, WA

Magical Wind

When the wind dances through your hair you can feel the magic in the air
As the wind blows the magic comes when the sunrises and falls
This magic can be felt through out your heart
You can feel something magical through ones soul
Which makes you want to dance as the wind blows when the sunrises and
falls
When one dances from sunrise to sun fall your heart follows how the
wind beats into your feet that follows the direction of the wind that
dances through your hair

Jessica Jo Hedin
Kent, MN

Wildfire

Monster licking its' chops,
it crackles, hisses and pops.
Tongues of red, yellow and blue
flicking about the ominous hue.
Born in lightening flash
with thunderous crash?
Created by evil hand?
Birthed by careless man?
Once unleashed it roars
even as the water pours!
It grow and grows and grows.
It glows and glows and glows,
while all it devours
increases its powers.
Running wild with the wind,
a trail of ash where it's been.
Moving without discretion,
so quick to change direction.
Forest and construction
falling to its' destruction.
It does not grow quiet
nor sleep the night,
leaving men crying
weary from trying
to stop the wild rampage
of this monster with no cage.

Edith Andrews Phinazee
Birmingham, AL

In the Seeking

The wind is calling to me, with the voice of a lover who has long gone. What she speaks inaudibly, I ascertain with an aching sense of wrong. She whines longingly to me, and I understand I should not be here. Her words kiss my ears sweetly, then beckon that I draw near.

My eyes are drawn to the earth, sullen from realizing she is lost. She goes silent a moment, watches my feelings toss. Then she howls, demanding as ever, and begins to silently cry. Her tears fall on my face, quiet again as she awaits my reply.

Her tantrum begins anew and she flails and scatters debris. My debate is over when she calls out for peace. She goes silent again and her tears stop flowing down. She waits. Silence.

I helplessly follow my compulsion to leap up and run to her. Knowing I will never find her, but unable to surrender. Our relationship is in the seeking. It always was.

Noah K. Traeger
Portland, OR

Who I Am

I've caused so much suffering

A man lost in a world of rage and pain
Questioning why I was brought into this world
A soul fighting for an identity

Buried in a hole I dug myself
An inescapable truth I had to face
Alone I climbed out of that hell
I emerged changed and driven

Life is beautiful
But I still pay for my sins
Unfortunately that's how life is
And I have become a better man for it

Self reflection is a hell of a mirror
To be able to change for the better is exhilarating
Live your life and become the person you were meant to be
We are all better than we think we are

Steve Kornutiak
Marysville, CA

Love My Demons

Can't escape my demons
Nothin' clear can come between 'em
Wanna fight them even though I can't see 'em

They make me wanna cry
See the fear in my eyes
Feel like I wanna hide
...but it's the demons keeping me alive

Madison Jones
Scituate, MA

The Day Our Family Was Complete

The day you wed my son I gained another child,
A beautiful daughter as you walked down the aisle,
Seeing the love on my son's face,
I knew at last he had found his place,
I'm so glad he found you and the girls,
Such a beautiful family in a changing world,
Four beautiful daughters and a beautiful wife,
Gaining you to our family has truly blessed our life,
From three to seven our family grew,
The wonderful day the two of you said "I Do."

Patty D. Cooksey
Trumann, AR

Homeless, Missing Child

One day as l was playing,
I wasn't scared and I did not care.
I listened to a stranger,
now I'm here but I don't know where.
Momma are you wondering?
Momma are you there?
Momma, I hear you crying.
I'm here but I don't know where.
Are you lonely too dear mother?
Do you hurt down deep inside?
Since that lovely afternoon,
I feel like your heart has died.
Well Momma,
Don't hurt no more because I been gone a long, long while.
You'll love again,
but don't forget your homeless,
missing child.

Thomas Chesley
Lake Forest, CA

An Ode to You

So much time has gone by since we all said goodbye.
We miss you still, we miss you most.
Words of wisdom, funny stories, and beautiful jewelry.
How we always love to remember your beautiful smile
    and contagious laugh.
As long as we are all here no one will forget.
Your voice is now ours.

Amber J. Dillard
Fitchburg, MA

The Moonlight

His voice goes through my mind and to my fingertips; when he talks not
only does his voice leave vibrations throughout my body,
it also makes me fall in love with him more and more, same with his
personality and who he is as a person. The water in the ocean is making its
way to the sand and the moonlight shines on my skin as the wind blows. I
know it's just the moonlight trying to catch my eye and get my attention,
but how am I supposed to give the moonlight all my attention when he's
the only person I can think about? How am I supposed to only focus
on the moonlight when his voice gives my body vibrations that end up
rushing through my body to my fingertips?

Hannah Snow
River Ridge, LA

The Hollow End

I'm standing upon this ground
This spot that aches my soul
A heavy heart bleeding slowly
A broken spirit tearing fast
Completely blank and numb
In the end with no closure
Injustice to my sorrow
What's done was done
Obligated to turn a blind eye

This growing seed of darkness
Left alone at sea of strangers
Yet with a continuing bloodline
But the black sheep and monster
Morning to nightfall
Day by day
A face well done to perfection
A smile that must be worn
This mask my forever cage
The silence of my screams.

Brittany Williams
Baltimore, MD

My Home

I love Tennessee just how it is,
No need to change, God made it his.
Behind our house, there are some trees,
When I run down the hill, I usually fall on my knees.

It rains a bunch one day,
But the next is dry as hay.
When fall finally hits the air,
I sit outside and act like I don't care.

One thing I love to do,
Is play outside while the sky is blue.
Watching birds fly around,
And listening to their beautiful sound.

Tennessee is my newest home,
Where my friends and I love to roam.

Faith Gabbrielle Franklin
Franklin, TN

Into the Woods

Come into the woods with me and smell the earth beneath your feet.
Here the sounds of nature call, come into the woods with me.
I go to find the strengths of my soul.
The deeper I walk in the forest floor,
the mind starts to clear and my souls fire glows,
the meaningless thoughts fade away.
The soul sets the pace as we walk together,
we are connected for ever and ever.
I feel myself coming out from within,
knowing my time has a limited end.
I am not scared for what is next.
I hear a familiar voice say, "Come home child with me
where your beautiful soul can always be free."
I looked behind and smiled .
I say to my soul,"Come walk with me that one last mile."

Grace E. Ohde
Athens, WI

Under Water

Under water I am
Swimming aimlessly
Yes, it is blue
So blue I've forgotten orange
The sun I have not seen
Only nights lacking stars
Clocks, there are none
Time stops not under water
I dream for the day
I swim to the surface
But outside this ocean
I see no land
There is no refuge
I cannot cross the surface
Under water I will be.

Eesha Thakur
Newtown, PA

You

You were wearing your hair differently
Carrying the air differently
The world began to stare differently.
At you.
You knew it too.
You saw the world three less than perfect.
You waged a battle without weapons
but knew that it was worth it.
With just your mind, advanced
With just your courage, shaking
You embraced the chaos knowing
A good mistake needed making.
You stared into the mirror
Unphased Unfathomed Unflinching
You prepared to kill the demon there as
A warning to the others not to come lurking.
Exhaustless you took the mantle
New eyes, new hair, new armor.
Faultless you screamed the mantra
"However far they went, I'll go farther."
Smirking, I turn away from you smirking.
It seems God forgot to tell you
When it was time to stop working.

Sirigrid Bennet
Edwardsville, PA

The Man Who Hung at Calvary

Everyone knows the man who hung at Calvary
Everyone knows he was crowned with a crown of thorns
Everyone knows he shed his blood for us
Everyone knows he gave his life for us
Everyone knows it's how it always had to happen
There was no escaping it
Because that's how it had to go
Everyone knows

Everyone knows the poor will be with us always
The rich get rich
But in the end the poor will be richer
For that's how it goes
Everybody knows

And everybody knows that the Great Tribulation is coming
Everybody knows that there will be a great falling away
Everybody knows that the believer
Is just a priceless relic from an era long ago past
Everybody knows we were condemned to a life of sin
But he said oh no
Now everybody knows
That salvation and repentance is the way to go

Cody Williams
Athens, AL

In My Head

You think you know about pain
Until you look in my head
I've been standing in the rain
As all my friends disappear

I've been on my knees praying
Oh God please make it clear
Should I continue to live?
Or should I just disappear?

I've been on this road
Just trying to find which way to go
I've been walking alone in the desert
Now I'm thinking it's my time to go

Demons are fighting
As it gets harder to breathe
Feel like I've gone blind
As it gets harder to see

In the end
No one cares about me
As i attempt to break
All these chains off of me

Have i finally given up?
Am i better off dead?
Only God knows the answers
As the battle continues all in my head

Ryan Cooke
Camden, OH

The Tape That Has Taunted

Press play: observe the pain that harms the heart.
Then rewind it back to the start.
Fast forward through all the muddled thoughts.
Pausing occasionally to connect the dots.

The memories that are always stained.

The pictures that will be perpetually ingrained.
The smile that is forever feigned.
The conscience that is continually chained.

The morose mind that has been haunted.

The tape that has taunted.

Marcie Wodlinger
Issaquah, WA

In One Hand Time's Pencil...

In one hand time's pencil, but in the other hand time's eraser,
And line by line, written events are erased, forgotten in history.
Read what love dictates, sweet thoughts of love,
before time's eraser turns words into forgotten dust.

Richard A. Barnes
Creswell, OR

A Poet's Mind

A poets mind is like a scribbly line
So sometimes I leave the world behind
To take a dive into my mind
A gift and a curse is what it is
Sort of like a divine bind.
Rain dancing on a slippery slope
Holding hands with intelligence and insanity
Making words say more than they do
Come and enter the realm of poetry
You'll see dark sounds and hear bright colors
A poets mind is like none other.
By taking language and removing its limits
Fluency and flexibility are creative conflicts
Manipulating words to give you a view
Through my own lens, use your soul to zoom.
Do you see what I see? Can you hear the wind?
Feel the downpour of sentences overflowing from within.
I want to escape but where would I go?
A poets mind... too deep to be shallow
Slightly anxious, wayward thinking
My heart takes pictures and to life, words bring them
Thinking close to the edge, submerged in my thoughts
Reality does not confirm what can't be bought.
A poets mind... distant. Full.
Although free from restraint, it's being constantly pulled.

Ebony J. McIntyre
Rochester, NY

Crooked Beauty

Amethyst jewels
Hung loosely on aged skin,
Dangling effortlessly against the
Faded background.
The vibrant life of color
Worn away by time.

Magenta lips
Moist with anticipation
Yet parched from display;
A swirl of words blended together,
Obscure ideas shaped by
Lines of expression.

Inspiration
Evident from
Tainted gold rimmed frames
To moon shaped canary silk.
Frosted strands of precision like
Smooth silver strokes
Of the artist.
Subtle hints of oil scents
and timelessness,
Stubborn fragrance captured by the years.

Sapphire skies
Seen from
Windows of the soul.
Eternal beauty
Set before the world.

Kate Marcus
Charlotte, NC

Never Give Up

When life gets tough, It's harder to survive
Trying not to cry as the days go by
With every step I take, every breath I make
I can see my mistakes
Time to change paths
Find who I am inside!
It's not going to be easy
But with God by my side, I will reach the sky!
Here's to new beginnings!
Opening a new door, it's right for sure
You never let me down
My faith is so high in the clouds
God here I am!
Giving my all to you
With you by my side, I will reach the sky
I have faith in you

Haley Hebert
Thibodaux, LA

Drifter

Obsidian oblivion - warm and wet.
Pressing on my palm while licking up my sweat.
Pinkish hues and an ancient inhalation;
slobber on my fingers with jumps of jubilation.

Wiggling, waggles - wanting scratches and kisses,
an uncontrolled tail whacking with near-misses.
Primal instincts kick in when his favorite ball is thrown;
Socks find new homes in places I've never known.

Dash! Clunk! CRASH! Careening down dark corridors.
Skid! Bang! THUD! Running into creaky old doors.
Landing on my lap, wide eyes begging for rubs -
There is no greater feeling than a dog's love.

Friday Bakhos
Naches, WA

Under the Water

Is this the silence that I've been waiting for
The silence that will one day sweep me off my feet
The peaceful abyss of sleeping under the horrid dreams of days past
Under the water that weights more than a ton and carries your sorrow
worries and guilt away on the boat made from your own mistakes

Jeffrey Deleon Vaca
Woodbridge, NJ

Waiting

I long for something I cannot have.
A longing that cleaves my heart,
threatening to shatter me
if I find no relief.
But there is none, no cure
for a searching and lonely heart
that longs to be loved.
Longing for a love that is so pure, the lilies blush for shame.
A love that is so patient, the caterpillars pause in constructing their
cocoons.
A love so gentle, the softest breeze halts in reflection.
A love so strong, so consuming, that even the wildfires give pause.
A love so whole, so complete, that the waters of the world tremble.
A love to fill the cracks and voids,
a love with cracks and voids for me to fill.
But it is not time. And so my heart
continues her lament of love, of pain;
continues to cleave its way to my soul,
my very self.

Sarah Catherine Neubecker
Canandaigua, NY

Shadow of a Hawk

The Red-tail Hawk flies over head,
but under the sun.
As its Shadow passes across the ground,
smaller animals run.
The Hawk is a hunter,
always will be.
That's Nature at its best,
a life that's free.
When the Shadow of a Hawk passes over;
birds fly for deepest cover.
Maybe there is something here,
the two-legged can discover.
On their own birds are busy bumping,
shoving each other;
for the best place to feed.
I've watched the same with two-legged;
chasing their vanity and greed.
Except when the Hawk's Shadow passes over them.
Then they start singing their favorite Hymn.
This is their greatest fear.
Even they get quite;
when the Shadow of a Hawk is near.

Robert Mica
Flatonia, TX

Bottled Up

Seeds of poems lay stashed
in her, sans time to sprout out
leaf by leaf.

She yearned to carve out
tiny slivers of time
'tween countless chores.

But then, was it time's lack
or writer's block
that held her back?

Every trick failed to work;
the ticking of the clock
almost made her choke.

They are nonstop,
the work and the clock;
they balked her lone hope.

Finally the fire in her heart
minted in its forge
a few fertile moments.

And a poem slowly germinated
like an oak out of an acorn,
like a cedar out of a seed!

Elsy Paulose Kalaparampath
Charlottesville, VA

Harpsichord Spectrum

Musical instrument, smooth tapping on keyboards.
Plectrum small yet strong, at trigger plucks accord.
Prologue etymology similitude, family feud.
Varying specific set of steps, a continuum continued.
Antiquity resonator pedals to dissipate pitch.
Scientifically optic wave in degrees, pillar arch rich.
I mean I have been running at an angel.
In this moment, menace me with bespangle.
Soundboard agriculture clavicebalum sculpture.
Keli nevel psalteries ketuvim, culture.
Eyelet, designed resonating elegance ensepulcher.
Light source continuous absorption according to prism.
Thee well said; dramatis personae dissimilitude schism.
I overlaid in elation with an pulchritudinous image.
Immeasurable immaculate imbue imagination envisage.
Prodigious birth born both, lyre to summer flowers.
Hands do touch, and palm to palm a kiss.
Maybe in Paris, a mans power.
Grace stumbled upon counsel in this hour.
Strings on bar chromaticism tonality, tower.
Seven hundred and forty nanometers visual field.
Transduction signals occipital lobe, interprets a build.
Activates levels plucked with chordophone fingers colloquially.
Parallel a cordes pincees a clavier perpendicularly.
Chamber ensembles a board.
Spectrum of harps as chords.

Dominique L. Watson
Washington, DC

In an Instant

Your life can change forever!
One critical error
One wrong decision
One unexpected incident

You might sense it coming
You might see it coming
Or you might be totally blind sided

The will to survive is an enormous power within
Panic and fear alarms your mind
You are in distress
It's fight or flight

Busted, broken, shattered
Your mind is exploding
The pain is excruciating

Time stand still
What happened

Help! Hurry!

There is a sudden shock then...
Everything fades to darkness

In an instant!

Carol Sue Dawley
Winnebago, MN

Crying for the Masses

Blinded
By your individual sadness
Consumed by hatred
Fuel for your deeds
Driven by your greed
Your infinite needs
Violent tendencies
They surround me
Tragic world in madness
We are all lost
In the sadness
Its time
To cry for the masses

Teresa Russell
Kansas City, KS

The Love Light

From birth, as you are born,
you are born with a light, a light as bright as the sun
As the years pass, the light in your soul is love, love for your family,
love for your friends, love for the world.
When your family and friends begin to disappear and fade to the other
side, your lovelight begins to dim.
Don't let your love light go out.

Troy Michael Harmon
Bonne Terre, MO

Reflections

She looks at her reflection in the window glass
A fading image of who she once was
Not a clear picture of who she is now
A few wrinkles around her eyes
She's a bit more plump
Her protected heart of love and kindness
That part of her will never change
Her hair sparkling essences of gray
The smell of her perfume lingers in the air
Her ruff hands shows signs of hard work
Her walk is a little less steady
She writes her beautiful stories and poems
Not requiring much thinking

Talent that flows like water bouncing off rocks in a creek
Her age has not changed her talent or creativity
She boasts her love for mystery and the unresolved
She holds her pen tightly as she gives her story its final twist
She calls it a night as she lays down her pen
She walks away from her desk feeling proud and content
Her work for tonight is finished.

Nellie Marie Seuss
Mountain Lake Park, MD

Let Freedom Seize!

Freedom is ringing!
Can't you hear them singing?
Freedom is rising!
The Paradigm Shifters are no longer hiding!
Freedom is coming!
Can't you hear them drumming?
Freedom is revolutionary!
This generation will bring truth to many!
Freedom is here to stay!
The skies have opened for this day!
Freedom is within you!
Change will be the breakthrough!
Let freedom be!
Let freedom seize!

Keonna Nelson
Philadelphia, PA

Hell

The heat charred my skin,
   until it peeled and came back thicker
The smoke burned my lungs,
   until I coughed up my heart
The hooves dug into my back,
   until bones broke and mended stronger
Their snickers and my screams rang in my ears,
    until the vibrations burst my eardrums and scarred my throat
    leaving me deaf to deprecation and unable to speak your name
The darkness weakened my eyes,
   until I could only see in black and white

Chloe Henderson
Bethel, OH

Grey Buildings

Cozy in the chaos that feeds the society.
Carefully disguised with a mask of propriety.

Just another faceless figure cast in the painting.
Swaddled by the noise like a baby in entirety.

Visibly secret and obviously hidden.
Some may take note but none would have written.

Talking is just waves and the bustle is just static.
Breathing, heart beating and foggily smitten.

Esme Cammarata
Oakland, CA

How I'm Feeling

Hair on my chest
blood in my eyes
in event of my demise
hope I can survive
Trying to fight to stay together
reliving the past praying for the better
always expecting the worse
goddam everything around me is a curse
In a world that's deceiving, I'm clearly receiving
People are saying common sense when they aren't even making cents
nothing feels the same playing this game

Angie M. Phillip
Port Saint Lucie, FL

To My Husband and His Lover

It's been a mess
a paralyzed, white-knuckled
sort of tragedy
that makes getting water-boarded sound like fun
And when we reach a decision that we can't make yet
all I want is to be loved by a lover who can't love back
Would you take my clothes off after work
so you can be mine for a little while?
No, send me into a spiral of disorganized thoughts
but we can't talk about it
shh
because this is starting over
Her and I are on the same coin
that you flip hastily between your fingers
who would've thought I would land face up
instead of drowning beneath the weight of a forbidden love
Who am I to come between?
So I'll beg you to release me
But as soon as I start to untie this knot
you pull me closer
and the promises stack up
like get-well-soon cards at a dialysis clinic
But let me stop here
because I'm sure you both are tired
and I haven't eaten yet today

Elizabeth Hunter
Portland, OR

That Spark in Your Eye

I met you when you were only five
And I'll never forget that spark in your eye
Your spirit so gentle; your personae so light
Like a beacon of hope on a warm summer's night

As you grew I watched you struggle with life
Yielding the urge to quarrel or fight
I knew then you were a gift from above
Brought to us as a symbol of love

Through your teens I saw you grow and struggle
Enduring the pain of life's affliction
I hoped then you could endure the world
And not succumb to your addiction

Speaking last night at the funeral home
I knew you'd returned; but would not be alone
You'd rejoined a place where there is only love
Your departure in peace on the wing of the dove

For some the world is too hard to face
You did your best and you did it with grace
I know you're in a much better place

I will remember you always and try not to cry
As I recall that spark in your eye

Corinne Frontiero
Wyandotte, MI

Our Soul

It was love at first sight, though it didn't happen at night I knew it was
meant to be.
A feeling like this made me feel such bliss. You're forever a part of me.
For the love that we shared both so unprepared, unable for unity.
But our soul knew better tried to force us together and gave us this entity.
Love really is blind when you feel and nevermind. True love is
unconditional you see.
Creative attempts to manipulate
because you think your way is so great.
This should cause you to realize
that when you fantasize
alone in your mind you disconnect the bind
that ties our soul
where split they should be whole
reunion in complete harmony.
It's hard to be away, sometimes it's tough to stay when you say things that
make me want to cry.
It's only us three in this reality
still I think we should try living out our dream life where I'm your happy
wife in our home by the sea.

Kristin Dunn
Fuquay Varina, NC

The Memory of You

It was contagious.
It billowed throughout the room.
Instant recognition of your presence.
Sometimes it came out guttural
Others it was whistle-like.
Your smile was a perfect accessory to it.
As the symptoms set in, the less freely it came.
It became more calculated and reserved.
Oh how I long to hear it one more time.
It drew me into you.
I'd sit enveloped in it while on our mission
To save princess Peach.
Now I'm shrouded in silence.
I reach for memories of the way
It transformed me out of sadness.
If they say laughter is the best medicine
You would be here.
Happy, Healthy.
Moonwalking to M.J.
Filling my silence with that big Andy laugh.

Amber Cannon
Marshalltown, IA

Snake

Nightmares. Demons. No help.
Lonely battles with not only myself.
They are powerful. But I'm so much
Stronger than this thing.
The snake that surrounds me is not silent anymore.
Easily distracted by things I keep missing.
How can this make any sense?
To another I'm delusional and possibly mad.
How come you chose to act like that?
Like you know all. Didn't she lie to you again?
Go for it. Honey and cinnamon.
The key is the cure to the heart of the sickness,
Yet you try and convince me the trap doesn't exist.
I'm sick? You're sick! Stop lying to me.
We are as sick as our secrets and I smell a disease.
Like the plague but invisible, carbon monoxide feels sweet.
I wonder if they'll be there when we finally meet.
The judgement is not character.
If you're impaired by abstinence.
All it takes to see them is one little kiss.
The snake gets older but never ages.
If you change nothing then of course
You won't go through changes.
The blind man can see beyond the fields he'll never view.
Your deafness is only silent to you.

Nichole Pittman
Odessa, TX

Who Am I?

Today is like no other, I finally abandoned all hope of life.
Bottom feeders they are every last person, but I am also person.
Or at least I was... person.
My choices can never be undone or forgiven, because that's the last thing I would want.
Carry the bodies of the dead and fling them off great heights a proper burial they do not deserve.
Hang the wife's by the collars and remove the eyelids of the spouse.
Feed the young to the animals.
True sanctuary can start to blossom when sacrifices are made.
This beating heart... this cursed beating heart has no place in my Heaven.
Can you hear the cries of the dead? they are happy I freed them.
Freed them from a false living and they thank me for it.
Not all endings are happy. Is that a bad thing?
Let me shut my eyes and embrace it.
Pure silence.
I was once person.
Now I am free.

Jeffrey Bellamy
Willowbrook, IL

The Taken

They roam the earth trapped,
Alive or dead and stuck;
While families and friends must adapt.

They used to be warm and safe with blankets wrapped,
Now no such luck;
They roam the earth trapped.

By our guilt and pain we are also entrapped,
From this cycle ourselves we must pluck;
While families and friends must adapt.

Kidnaps, suicide, and murder has happed,
Anger, pain, and suffering has struck;
They roam the earth trapped.

Everything changed when someone snapped,
People getting more amuck;
While families and friends must adapt.

In these times hate is inapt,
Love will make us all unstuck.
They roam the earth trapped,
While families and friends must adapt.

Elizabeth Mae Prater
Berea, KY

Renamed Again

As we hydroplane across deserted skies we reach for anything close to a
horizon,
A gull stretches out her tired wings, drinking water off a cloud.
She tells me who we are.
A leaf in the distant sky eliminates any question in our mind.
We are what we are not,
and we cannot become what we have not been before.
Yet we are always what we can become;
reaching for ourselves we fall down into the rabbit hole,
incomplete and whole.
Immediately we dismember our spirits and our souls and cling to the wing
of the gull, hoping she could fly us back to the deserted sky,
but she denies our request and fills up our cup while telling us stories of
the other us.
Scared to the brink of reality, we jump to the edge of our seat while the
gull mocks us for even thinking there is an edge to our seat.
Unamused we laugh and cry and sing and shout and in that instant we are
born and we are forgotten,
lost to the winds that echo through the stars and later found by the foam
of the ocean waves
crashing down on the dunes of your mind's melodious mountains,
only to trickle down to the rivers that feed the falls that we drink from
every single day,
subtly hoping one day we may find out who we were the day before.

Israel Orstrom
Portland, OR

Roaming Blunders

We all lose
our sense of direction
The map
falls into the fire,
the ink fades,
we took a wrong turn
and didn't pay attention.
Regardless.
Even in the muck
not all is lost.

We may grow weary,
but by taking the
off beat path
we gain strength.
We gain perspective.
We learn more
about ourselves and how
we grow.
So even though we may
find ourselves
desperate for clarity,
being misdirected
helps our identity.

For no matter where we travel
we can always find home.

Auna J. Lundberg
East Wenatchee, WA

Through the Window

My window is dull by resplendent sun rays
reflecting only visions from my mind's eye.
A prism of random images, flashing faces
of those that came before thee,
and those who would be...still,
alone in my chariot of wheels,
I am subjugated!
As the sun's rays diminish
a vision far-off, barely distinguishable,
yet dark and daunting -
It's what I feared and longed for...

Gary Wayne Enos
Hayward, CA

I'm Not Afraid

I'm not afraid to die but I am afraid of the dark and why lies within it
I'm not afraid to die but I am afraid of growing old alone
I'm not afraid to die but I am afraid of failure
I'm not afraid to die but I am afraid of not fulfilling my dreams
I'm not afraid to die but I am afraid of being unhappy
I'm not afraid to die but I am afraid of change
I'm not afraid to die but I am afraid of the realities of life
I'm not afraid to die but I am afraid I will be forgotten
I'm not afraid to die but I am afraid of losing myself
I'm not afraid to die but I am afraid of just existing and not living...

Sidqieh Nowal Salim
Clanton, AL

Till Her Last Breath

Gently awoken
T'was twilight
He, somber
Dark
A stranger looking into her eyes
Poised in a runner's stance for flight
Again
So many agains
The count lost
Always indescribable pain
Picked up pieces crumbling
Patterns written in the stars
He would return
Heart begins to mend
Land mines strategically placed
On fool's day he came
The fool protected
Sanity held by a loose thread
No more agains
Only pure love
Till her last breath

Gabriela Vuichoud
Cave Creek, AZ

Beyond One's Own Self

A world without evil is not one with intrigue,
Nor a world of only joy, for it bores me.
A world of light would draw me to cast a shadow,
And a world without turbulence would be woefully still.
A world of sunshine and rainbows is not one I fancy,
For I would only desire the heavens to grow heavy with sorrow.
A world beyond one's own self is a world of mine;
A world where self overflows into the world,
Flooding past its corporeal bonds.
A world where limits matter not, and conventions lay deceased.
I dream of a world where doubt is laid to rest and potential rises anew;
I dream of a world where one's actions are immune to causality;
I dream of a world where reality is but an idea,
Molded by the beholder.
I dream of a world of:
Unstoppable pursuits,
Eternal dreams,
Boundless potential,
Soul devouring desire,
And impossible imagination.
I dream of a world beyond one's own self.

Malik Naloev
Union, NJ

Missing My Yellow Acacia

I cannot explain it
Smiling is impossible
Thinking about it hurts
Hearing my acacia laugh makes me happy... for awhile
I think about all the good times
Wishing I can go back and redo it
Knowing what I know now
Finally being happy
I wanna say sorry
And cry
The world will never know but me
Or maybe it will
Someday we can go back
To where it all started
Taking you with me
In my heart
I'm stupid to believe in a flower
The pure yellow of it makes me sick
And I'm tired of trying
Hopeless
Never will it be the same
Because true hell will rise if my flower finds another
My heart will break
My soul will melt
 My yellow acacia

Nae Chanel Mazique
Kent, WA

Beneath the Moon

So lucid with her words and fluent with a pen,
but she was never very good with sorting what lies within.
The secrets of her heart or the meaning of its dealings,
Or even with understanding the simplest of feelings.
Life made more sense to her underneath the moon and stars,
The way it all connected stitched together her scars.
The glory of the moon and how it fell and how it rose,
How it holds it all together with the secrets that it knows.
It knew her heart had been broken, but was beating just the same,
It'd listened to her thoughts, and never once called her insane.
The moon stimulated the tides of her soul and of her mind,
And guided her to understand the feelings that she'd find,
When she looked into the glow tonight, she understood what her heart
had said,
And learned that her hearts feelings, never belonged inside her head.

Jen A. Ruch
Newton, NC

Inherent Catharsis

I'm not a maverick, I'm not who you think, I gave everything away, and now you trust all that I take, I want to be safe with you, I want all the same things you do, and now I'm falling apart leaving you

Time to let go, time for one of us to know, watching you with someone else, I can't shed a tear, I'm as hard as the words that left you cold

Memories of different dreams, it's cathartic looking back at all those silent screams, I can't stop now, what I told you I was supposed to be is creeping up on me, and now all I can do is watch you leave

Time to let go, time for one of us to know, watching you with someone else, I can't shed a tear, I'm as hard as the words that left you cold

I'm not a maverick

Derick Mitchell Matthews
Lawrenceville, GA

Mystery

Can you solve this mystery,
meant only for you and me? -
A mystery so concealing, about a past love that enveloped me?
Can you solve my mystery, why I left so long ago? -
Why my heart was devoid of love, my betrayal the final blow?
Can you solve this mystery?
Look not at yonder name.
Look not for explanation, for in riddle concealed my game.
Can you solve this mystery?
Well, find me if you care!
For, my heart is sore from bleeding,
though I'll never desert you, I swear.

Zoe Angela Blackmon
Sweetwater, TX

L.O.A.N.

It's an emergency; I need a LOAN.
I need the LOAN as soon as possible.
This LOAN I need will help me in this dire situation.
This situation I am in is heart brokenness.
This LOAN I need does not have to do anything with money.
This LOAN that I am asking for doesn't need a co-signer or require a
credit check.
This day and age, I believe everyone need and deserves this LOAN.
This LOAN that we all need is "Love Over All Negativity."

Derhone Brown
Baltimore, MD

Lost

Sweet child sitting under the weeping willow tree.
Tears fall and no one comforts you.
Your mother is gone.
Due to a person who sits on his throne and tells lies.
Sweet little girl don't be sad.
You have so much to live for.
Too much blood has been shed already.
Little girl who sits under the weeping willow tree.
Tears fall hitting the ground like angry drums.
Come home little girl come home.
You do not wish to have your mother's fate.

Maria Juarez
Live Oak, CA

Broken Trust

The shadows dwell where darkness lies.
With them their friend doubt complies.
Causing pain and misery for everyone else to see,
The past you can't seem to just let it be.
Her actions torture your mind and soul,
Causing for your many thoughts to troll.
The shadows is where they seem to stay.
That doubt likes the darkness to come and play.
In your mind no trust can build,
For the past is what keeps that thought fulfilled.
Fights and arguments, they burst out.
In the end your relationship is whats keeping from that doubt.

Krystal Thurston
Clarksummit, PA

A Poem I Wrote for Someone No Longer in My Life

Her eyes are autumn's last leaves,
Fallen down to grace the earth with her presence.
In everything she has kindness,
Spreading her love with every breath.
She, a sweet late spring flower,
Bares beauty for all to behold.
Her smile is sunshine incarnate,
And I, undeserving, am lucky enough to gaze upon that sunlight.
She is soft spring air,
Breathing life into every room she enters.
Her voice is first birdsong after winters dormancy,
Melting my heart at its sound.
Her laughter is the embodiment of joy,
Encapsulating me in moments of pure bliss.
Her boisterous beauty is only outdone by the beauty of her soul,
And everyday I count my lucky stars in all their numbers, that I am
fortunate enough to have crossed paths with that very soul.

Chris Adkins
Oak Harbor, WA

Loving You

When the valley
rises to the sea,
When the moon always
stays Harvest full,
When the Autumn leaves
do not fall,
When the snowflakes
lose their sparkle,
That's when I'll stop
loving you.

Patricia Jean Carter
Wellesley, MA

Sea Dreams

Warm and fast the wind travails,
bathing me, as the sea
in lovely swaths of waves and time.
willing this to last...far and away.
Green and Gray and Blue, the ocean
with kisses of soft, white, frosting crests.
Rosy is the sky, as the sun desires to impress before its nightly
slumber.
The horizon, the edge of the world,
A line ruled by God...
murmurs its endless song of the deep.

Mary Beth Davila-Aponte
Winter Springs, FL

Troubled

Who is she to blame?
A girl troubled, yet sane.
Inside a good heart she had.
It wasn't like her to lose everything she had, how sad.
Little by little the time flew by.
Erasing a path she so carefully designed.
Becoming a road that led her to trouble.
Now she is stuck and depressed.
Eaten by sorrow.
Influenced by a demon, so strong, so mad.
It swallowed her pride and left her to die.
It stole her soul, raped her mind.
Took over her thoughts and cut away her time.
Now she is left with little or nothing to do, so she continued to use.
It's become who she is.
She has no good left to turn back around.
She has only the miles in front of her to do what she planned.
Try to salvage what remains.
Repair what she can

Miranda Ridenour
Coulterville, CA

Subtle Influence

Influences
They get you in the mouth and brain
Change the way you think so that you think the same
Influences

They make your talking bad with swears
All your holy beliefs, that belief is stripped bare

Influences
Add songs to your playlist
So many artists, now your playlist is their A-list
Influences

Barely know that they are there
Change your whole life, then disappear into the air

Influences
They make you think your thoughts are less
Slowly convince you that their way of thinking is best
Influences

Change the path you walk, change the way you talk
So that you can't walk the walk

Jordan Rex Alexandre
Randolph, MA

Moonlight

A moonlit stroll
A soft candle glow
Gentle words
Falling like snow
Gathering around
With a whispering sound
A light breeze blowing
Like sweet laughter flowing
A butterfly kiss
A heart left pounding
The touch of skin
Warm and soft
A room now spinning
To the sound of him singing
Lights now dim
All I see is him
Wishing time would stop
And the moon would never drop

Mea Katkus
Wasilla, AK

The Best in Need for 2020

An important election is due in 2020.
Now, what is needed in 2020.
For those eligible voters in 2020.
The important need is to actually vote in 2020.
To boycott a vote by not voting in 2020
will not solve an important duty that needs to be done in 2020.
By voting, you achieve a right to criticize a bad office holder in 2020.

Alan Leake
Bennington, VT

I Got You

I remember how you told me our love affair had to end.
We couldn't be lovers we could only be friends.
I was so afraid I was not able to sleep at night.
I had to do something to make you see the light.
I was so broken hearted I couldn't really think.
I tried to make you go away with just one more drink.
But you stayed on my mind no matter what I tried.
Finally I gave up and just layed down and cried.
But I kept the faith hoping you would understand.
And see how much I cared and take my hand.
I tried to be funny,used all the cool lines.
Hoping you'd come back,it didn't take much time.
And now we are together,you are so much of my life.
I'll never forget the day we became husband and wife.

Marty L. West
Bremen, AL

What's Left of Me?

It's all said and done
His imperious prideful soliloquies, that, he "won"
Make sure she settled with none
No more home to run
Her precious effects packed, towed and gone
Affliction from an abandoned heart left to be alone

What's Left of Me?
I'm miscellany storage of reminders attached with a fee
An unjust lesson in humility
An empty feel of bobbing in a vast sea
Heart fluttering from anxiety, no Haven for me

Whispers from within, barely audible to count on
It's not said or done and Karma has really won
This adversity you faced is not your future from now on

What's Left of Me?
My babies who love me
The strength and wisdom gained through calamity
An inner voice with pertinacity
An ex-husband with culpability
My certainty in a future of Amity to be.

Amanda Josephine Riles
Irvine, CA

Tight Rope

We start out on a tightrope,
With an up and down slope.
We start out on small hope,
Not knowing how to cope.

Down and up on that rope,
We sway to and fro.
Our eyes all aglow,
Our eyes pained in outflow.

Around and around along that rope,
How it twists,
How it tightens,
How it becomes a noose,
Ever to be loose?

Sophia Clara Nagy-Rizzuto
Beaverton, OR

I Can't Believe It

On my knees again,
I'm begging the lord please.
Hold me in these times my soul is in need.
The clouds open to me, and a hand stretches to me.
I heard a voice say "I'm taking you home right where you was supposed to
be." I will encourage you with my word, because I feel no pain. Filled with
his word, I saw my spirit drift away.

Destruction can be easy too; those who lost their way,
but if you just hold on everything will be okay.
I said "Lord oh Lord, my soul's in need.
It seems everywhere I go the devil tends to follow me".
I hate those who hurt me, despise those who curse me.

Silence came over me. Tears flowed down my face.
"Oh ye of little faith, why don't you trust me?
I'm the alpha and the omega, the first and the last.
Without me there is no you so stop making this all about you."
I'm still a kid. What am I supposed to do?
"The devil lies to you. Trickery is his game," he said to me.
"Believe in me" then His hand stretched to me.
He said, "Everything will be okay." I cried once again.
I just couldn't believe God took time to talk to me.

Robert Zedekiah Young
Saint Mary's, GA

Badge of Honor

Those who wear badges, number quite a lot
Spirited individuals constantly sought
They work from patrol cars and other areas on their feet
This is their livelihood, this is their beat
They do this job because they care
Risk everything, face danger, even dare
To protect the innocent, catch those who are not
These are our heroes, now being constantly shot
Help them in the job that they do
The next one needing their help, may just be you

Ted J. Bauer
Sedalia, KY

Thoughts of You

Do you feel the rain
Does it touch your soul
How do you feel inside
Oh do you know
Its so special as the rain
When your around I feel no pain
Pure and clean like a dream
The rain can make a mind
Feel so relaxed and free
To be like honey to a bee
Or like leaves to a tree
You are so special to be for someone like me

Charlotte Diana Brummett
Bellville, TX

Weaver

Spider weaves the worlds
Catching us before we hit
Dirt filled paths
Tracing the lines of a figure
Long forgotten by some,
Always remembered by her-
In the web of daughters
She holds the eye for sight unseen

Delilah Ray Miske
Pottsville, PA

Yes I Do

I really love you; yes I do.
People wonder what I see in you.
I see love and the stars above.
Hoping you see the same in me.
The day will come when we'll be as one.
You'll put your arms around my hips
and I will kiss your tender lips.
But until that day I hope you'll stay
and our love will never fade away.
We'll share the good times and the bad
and remember all the joys we had.
The only guy for me is you.
I really love you; yes I do.

Melissa L. Burciaga
Madera, CA

Voicing for Souls

Sometimes
we hide in dark corners
because the light burns
and some people mourn
for us, the depressed
but they will never understand
the hardships of force
or scarrs
never will they get us
but, do we truly get ourselves?
for we are shadows
hidden or hiding
and we need to stop
our hardships make us strong
and valient
we are survivors
of the hot, lonely desert
we need to be a voice
for souls like ours
this prison will hold us no more
so stand
and be the voice
for voiceless souls
who are like you

Kataya Chelise Jackson
Millville, UT

Daisy

Pure yet tainted with pain
Hated yet Loved the same
Painted your petals a blood red so tell me daisy.....
Why must you hide your pain?
Pure as snow yet dark as hell
Like a daisy pure yet cold
Tell me the secrets that you hold
Eyes full of sorrow
Cells to your heart .
Please Daisy Tell me what is wrong
Pure yet Tainted with pain
Petals drip a blood red painting her surroundings as deep as her pain.
No one ever asked maybe if I loved her the same.
Sweet Daisy
Dear Daisy
Clean those bloody tears away let me wash the pain away.
Sweet Daisy
Dear Daisy
When will your pain go away?

Maria Fernanda Delacruz
Irving, TX

Valentine's Day (A Golden Shovel)

After Langston Hughes poem "Suicide Note"

> "The Calm
>   Cool Face of the river
>   Asked me for a Kiss"

I wanted her to send me the
world on a platter, calm
in substance and cool
as her beautiful face.
Instead she sent photos of
our life together in the
ever-changing flow of the river.
Sanguine and in love, I asked
her to marry me,
and waited in anticipation for
what seemed like eons, but only a
moment ... for that magical kiss.

Allen Smuckler
Sarasota, FL

Failure

My life is a stage and
I'm the main character who dies
in the end
is where I shall meet my fate-
forever meandering
until the evanescent shadow of my non-consolatory
life of which
I always seem to fall
when I get to the top because I make the same
mistakes
are lessons that I hope to learn from, that should
keep me from doing the same thing
Twice
I have sung my last song as the lights begin to die
Down,
down, down is where I'm going because
I forgot my lines—who I am
I to save the play and adlib, be fake, and die
a thousand deaths because I have
Failed myself.

Samantha Victoria Paz
Camarillo, CA

Better Days Are Coming

In the belly of the beast i undoubtedly take a seat
Though i thought this ride would be sweet
It crazy 'cause all i feel is hurt, pain, and defeat;
Nevertheless i figured this would cease.
But not until broken hearts and cries to the lord have been put at ease
In the midst of the storm, Lord give us faith and peace to go on
I drop to my knees and ask God to bring all madness to the light and
assure us that everything is gonna be alright
Never thought I'd see a day where my family just constantly fights
On a unknown quest through this thing called life
Lord make Carry strong as he continues to pull through
on a path through a stormy night
Lord bring our *entire* family back and continue to hold us tight.
The pain we have is deeper than what's shown in plain sight
but, Lord, we need you more and more each day and night.
We are a family built on love and togetherness.
Our ancestors would've never stood for this dreadful disaster.
The devil is busy but we all know the almighty Master;
He will fix it and bring an end to this even now and forever after.

La'niece Brittani Pierce
Lexington, KY

The Argument

manically determined
to belief in
All of Nothing
while
vehemently insistent
that such
popular putrescent philosophy
is
(contrary to prevailing reality)
progressive ideology.
wielding acronymous verbiage
in veiled attempts
to disguise
a paltry googled intelligence
impregnated with abhorrence
to Truth
to Life
to Common Sense.

Robin Harkey Bratton
Troup, TX

Humanity

Humanity is the human race which includes
everyone on earth. It's the word for qualities
that make us such as kindness, mercy, sympathy
but most of all love.
Humanity is important in growth of mankind
and trust on each other. Show kindness,
have mercy on your fellowman, be empathetic
towards the hurtful and share your love as God
has done for you.

Margaret Hope
Terre Haute, IN

Magic

I feel as though there's magic in the air
It's drifting about from nearly everywhere
It tickles the senses & entices the soul
It intrigues the young & reminds the old
It dances playfully among bodies at rest
It plucks at the heartstrings within the chest
It carves its initial within every open mind
It moves forward, pauses & then rewinds
It sprinkles concepts & ideas to those willing to receive
It is boldly honest & never does deceive
I feel as though there's magic in the air
It's drifting about from nearly everywhere

Jessica Comer
Butler, PA

Catharsis

Greed and jealousy,
a lesser's mind.

Adoration and tenderness,
a mother's touch.

Rage and hostility,
a fighter's fists.

Inquisitive and inspired,
a writer's soul.

Hate and love,
a madman's heart.

Madelyn Roberts
Louisville, KY

A Gift

Sitting on my porch in the morning breeze
as time ticks ahead towards autumn-colored leaves.
Beautiful yellows, oranges, and reds
blanketing the hills for miles ahead.
What a gift is given for all to see.
Mother Nature at her best for you and for me.

Liza Marie Ballard
East Brookfield, MA

Buried Inside

Crack the glass with bloody knuckles
Wacked   slammed   bled
The unsung hero, the negligent mother, falling apart in discontent
Hanging by a thread
How hard it must be to love your son, who waits for you, with an open
heart, heavy full of lead.
Anger of unknowing, happiness in lying
Smiles of a dying mother, unshed tears of a son
Looking back at me, a face I dare not see.
The untold stories of a childhood
How convincing you were, liquor in coffee cups, drinking through my
innocence
But always sober in time for the neighbors to be over
In life and in death, they're tears will only provoke her
She's gone but I'm still stuck with myself
My body and soul covered in scars
The mirror shows me what I wish not to see
The dripping from the holy faucet
In lieu of my sockets, the holy faucet drips tears for her, below that large
glass.
I don't want you here.
Stop reminding me of my fears.
Stop reminding me of the stories I don't want to hear.
Stop reminding me I never had her near.
I don't want to be reminded any longer.
Now I can not bury the fury brewing inside
You are always by my side!
Why won't you go away!
Wacked   slammed   bled, hanging by a thread.

Hannah Lily Chaffin
San Luis Obispo, CA

Heartbreak/Friendship

We were supposed to be best friends
To the very end
We have our ups and downs
Our laughter and frowns
I would ask you what was wrong
You kept singing the same song
That you were fine
But I was blind
You let them hurt you
Was I the fool
You were quiet and went with their flow
I think you were trying to give me hints but I was so slow
Now you're away
I wish you could stay
But this is your choice
You need to find your voice
You can't keep going down this road
Why have you turned so cold
I feel this is heartbreak I feel our friendship is no more
You didn't let me in you hurt me to my core

Raven M. Villafranco
Harlingen, TX

I Waited

I Waited
Years have passed
No word about her husband.

"Missing in Action"

Her heart tells her he is alive.
But everything else says he has died
As she looks at his picture-taking her wedding ring off and placing them together.
With tears running down her face
In a soft voice, you could hear her talking to him.

My Darling,

I waited for you for such a long time,
Every night I prayed for you to come back to me,
It was not to be.
For now, I will say Goodbye
The day will come when we will see each other again.
Laying the picture and the ring in a drawer

She knew it was forever.
But would it be?

Tammy L. Carter
Galax, VA

In the Presences of My Mind

Diamonds falling from the sky
Seeing rainbows in my eyes.
Landscapes sway like a wave
Colors saturates all the mind.
Swirling drift through a cloud
Colors flawless vibrant abound.
Undulating flowing blue skies
Mind soars as the sun warms.

It floats as if on a gently breeze
Like many feathers aloft to see.
A roundabout course is the way
For colorful sights trail and flow.
Best part of this trip has begun
And gone as soon as it arrives.
My mind is taking me to places
Where no one has been before.

Patterns of color upon the wall
For me to see, smile and fly by.
Swirling and shaping about into
That which only the minds sees.
Presences of a mind exists for all
No one can see inside mine but me.
It will always take me everywhere
Or simply leave me where I be.

Sheilah Say
San Diego, CA

Pain What's Up

Pain what's up
You never seem to leave
I'm use to you hanging on me
Like a shirt to a sleeve
through you some people
Can't but I can breathe
When you go away a little
I be like why did it leave
Your related to me
Like family of course
You hurt me like
A marriage that's divorced
I don't trust them
Like I trust you
Through their lies
You stay true
So what's up pain
What's up with you
Talk to me now
Make me cry
I'm not the one that's gone question you
And ask you why
I'll just receive you
Cause you never pass
Me by

Quiana Nikita Beco
Hawthorne, CA

Broken Heart Syndrome

Heartbreak may come in many forms
Some don't even notice it
It can be the feeling of dejection
when you find out someone close to you has passed
It can be the feeling of embarrassment
when they say they don't feel the same way
It can be the feeling of regret
when you forgot to say "I love you" before they left
It can be the feeling of misery
when the paycheck wasn't as big as you'd hoped for
It's the feeling of pure suffering
when the heartstrings in your chest won't stop pulling
Sometimes people stop it themselves to save their own selfless mind
"Stop being so sad and cheer up already"
"It's been months, why are you still sad?"
Heartbreak hurts
Mankind has tried to find a way to break this evil curse
A tightness in the chest
A difficulty breathing
The feeling of a true heart attack
"Broken heart syndrome" is what they call it

Cora Ruth Nath
Mechanicsville, IA

Consequences of Tentative Waters

Wading on the rocky shores of her temptation
Trying to steady the foundation
Swaying back and forth
My unwillingness to abort

Testing the waters of woe
The deliberation unending between friend and foe
What to trust, what to omit
Oh god, can I resist?

Maybe just one touch
I should not think of her this much
Maybe just one kiss
Do I dare be heedless?

The ever darkening sea passionate beneath me
Teaming with life and possibility
Mysterious and fulfilling
If only I am willing

I should jump and submerge
The risk is too great, I should diverge
To restrain or submit
I must be a hypocrite

Drowning in unrequited love
Is that something I'm deserving of?
What would I say?
Oh.. she floated away

Mary Peyton McKinney
Shreveport, LA

I Am Not Blind

I am blind
but yet I see
I feel, you see,
instead of see.
I am blind
people pity me
but they don't know
I've been set free
from visual judgments, visual loves,
the faulty gauges that mislead us;
facial expressions that so often belie
the person beneath and what's inside.
I am sentient, I am potent
I perceive instead of see
I am cognizant, I am puissant
because my eyes have failed me.
Make no mistake,
there is so much
in every voice, in every touch
in this darkness for me to find
of what counts in life—
I am not blind.

Sue Aldridge
San Anselmo, CA

Mystery Man

Many caught my eye but I pursued only him,
The tall mystery man who needed to be unraveled,
Time spent on the mystery man was not dim,
He had culture and was well traveled.
A militant man who'd rather listen than speak,
Somewhat older than his twenty three years,
A man who made me feel giddy and weak,
Out of my comfort zone conveyed many fears.

He, the teacher had appeared before me,
I, the student was ready to learn,
Unsure of what my future would be,
My love and affection the man had to earn.

Our homes were an ocean apart,
A life with him could be risky,
He captured my one true heart,
And made me really frisky!

He is like the bamboo that bends,
A rich heart under a poor coat,
We became life long friends,
My peaceful, loving, fearless now husband I dote.

A life lived for others is a life worthwhile,
Happiness, fulfillment, connection and meaning,
Be sure to notice my infinite smile,
For I am the wise one who is beaming!

Kim Remyn
Lake Alfred, FL

Come Eden

Long will I suffer,
In gratitude will I burn,
In triumph will I break
this enduring mortal coil.
In final, blessed peace
never to dwell here, again.

Heather Dawn Grove
Canton, OH

Love and Sunsets

I chased love like a kid chasing the ocean waves
I ran out to greet her, wide-eyed and excited
Only to find that once the excitement wore off
All I felt was cold
Left alone with the aching in my bones of loneliness
And regretting ever letting myself sink so deep

I watched her leave as if watching the sunset
Only realizing after the light was gone
That I was afraid of the dark
Still, I keep my eyes on the horizon
Hoping that perhaps one day the sun will rise
And that a sunset won't mean a forever goodbye

Rebecca Jennalynn Rightnour
Modesto, CA

Jesus

Flowers which are Gods to the ants,
With flapping arms of leaves in the wind.
Holding a warm scent to come again.

Marsha Gaide
Quincy, MA

My Soul Has a Body—Not the Other Way Around

My soul has a body not the other way around,
It will still be alive when this shell is in the ground,
It's my own special spark that makes me the person that I am,
Some say it's random chance and some say it's a plan,
It has to use this body to live in just one place,
Without it there's no limits not even time or even space,
My soul has a body not the other way around,
One day it will be free again and for now it must be bound,
To live a life as a mortal just to find my place in it all,
Knowing life is a gift to me even with the chance that I may fall,
Not knowing which way to turn when trouble comes my way,
I always stay strong and face it head on until a brighter day,
There's no need for me to wait for proof to be found,
My soul has a body not the other way around

Marc Adrien Patenaude
Starks, ME

Hope

People tell me to
Fly and reach out for my dream
As they break my wings

Yeeun Lee
Cupertino, CA

My Journey

My journey's all inside now,
No more outward quests.
No more mountains need I climb
Or windmills need I best.

My journey's all inside now,
I'm on my way back home.
In a world that's empty and confused
No longer will I roam.

My journey's all inside now,
I hear his voice afar.
His patient love is drawing me
Beyond the silver stars.

Michael Craig
Warren, MI

Little Sun

Little sun little sun can you tell me how the world begun
It begun when I was very young
And when I was one I had a lot of fun
And when I was two I had something to do
And when I was three I took a little pee
And when I was four I went on the floor to watch t.v.
And when I was five I was still alive
And when I was six I picked up sticks
And when I was seven I thought it was heaven
And when I was eight it was just great
But when I was nine it was just fine
And when I was ten I did it again
And that's the way the world begun when I was very very young
But now that I got a lot older I got a little bolder but that's another
rhyme for next time

Cherry Marie Stone
St. Helens, OR

This World

I have lived, not very long.
But long enough to learn and see,
What the Earth's creatures can do to help me.
They have taught us many things,
Things that helped us come to be.

Things that help us learn and grow,
To expand our horizons and come to know,
They teach us now in ways we do not see,
Like a young dogs loyalty.

I have lived, not very long.
But something I have learned to see,
Is the way a young horse looks at me,
With Grace and power and a hint of curiosity.

These creatures placed here on this Earth,
We're put here for you and me.
To help us learn and come to see,
The way this world was meant to be.

Korynn Laughlin
Phillipston, MA

A New Color

I stand at the edge of society's grasp
In my black and white attire
Reality never meets media
It's stuck on trends and desire.

A new color is what society needs
And with a little paint here and there
Some strokes of a brush can do the trick,
Paint over the hatred, jealousy and pain,
A Mona Lisa painted way too quick.

Why a Mona Lisa?
Because we just cover up the pain with a smile,
all the while in denial
Because nothing is on file.

Let's stop painting in the grey scale
And give the people what they need
A beautiful garden could grow
If you just plucked out the deadly weed

Another kid shot in his own hallway
And society only grows duller,
no more black and white perspectives,
so how about a new color?

Nya Janelle Smith
Tampa, FL

Bird on My Wrist

The bird on my wrist.
Flying forever,
Soars through the sky,
as free as can be.

Me
I'm on the ground.
I feel like I'm walking through cement.
Looking up to the sky,
As chained down as can be.

Longing to be free,
Looking into the sky.
I see the bird,
I begin to soar high

I'm set free,
By a bird,
A sparrow,
Or an eagle.

The bird on my wrist,
Was the one who set me free...

Katharine Elizabeth
Clay Township, MI

Snowfall

She held on until the snowfall
She had lived many winters pass
This one had arrived late
Mother nature sets her own time
I recall her smile, eyes that flickered like candlelight
There is only so much sorrow that anyone can hold
The weight becomes unbearable, the snow for borrow
It won't last
The freeze will break like a fever
It makes no wager; sets no plans

Robert R. Kinerk
Seattle, WA

To Whom It May Concern

We pass each other by without a glimpse, without a hi.
You probably wouldn't notice me, even if I tried.

It's almost torture knowing what I know and keeping it all inside.
But I have to keep trying, even though I am denied..
Each passing glimpse, I try harder and harder
just to find the perfect conversation starter.

Time and time again I fail; if only I had the courage to tell.

Irene J. Cline
Mooresville, NC

Repetitious

I find myself racing to work
To a job that can't even pay rent
Between the breaking and gassing footwork
I eat on the go with my headphones blaring
drowning out the hum of morning traffic
weaving in and out of lanes quite daring
Once free of the congestion I am for now, alone
Is this what my life shall be?
Near fatal misses, coffee stains, music my only company
Will one day I to become part of that traffics debris?
Mediocrely placed in a 'rat race' I charge on
What is the prize I'm chasing?
Time, Money, the hope of achieving The Freedom
The Privilege of 'The Good Life'
Paying with part-time, dollar menus, a gas hungry car
To play house with a husband I do not have
To eat brunch with friends I do not have time for
Or any other 'The Good Life' luxury I cannot obtain
Because running from five-year-old school loans
Credit card debt and parental roommates, is in vain
An Infinity Mirror of my life
A repeating insanity, show me how to break the glass
Slow down, use a napkin, roll down the window
Is there a prize if I come in last?

Jessica Hunter
Baker, FL

The World Is Dark

The world is dark and I stand alone
No blinding light
No burning sun
No bustling crowds
Just me to atone

A booming silence that hurt my ears
No gossipy whispers
No jeering laughs
No cracks of bones
Just the sound of my tears

I feel nothing above, nothing below
No muddy dirt
No scratchy nails
No shards of glass
Just the rub of my toes

I remember the light, the noise, the touch of a knife
I remember the sight, the ache, the pain inside and out
I remember the calm, the relief, the smile of content
Here, not there, is where I belong

Where the world is dark and I stand alone

Tanya Lertpradist
San Antonio, TX

Time

Tick- tock, tick - tock
The clock strikes one
She begins to walk

Tick - tock, tick - tock
The clock strikes two
She begins to talk

Tick - tock, tick - tock
You blink for only just a second
She is growing independent

Tick - tock, tick - tock
You wish for time to slow down
She is all grown up
Tick - tock, tick - tock

Jaelynn Davis
Chula Vista, CA

Unfurling

I am a single vessel
Standing alone in a desert
With no sky and no sand
There is only one moment
That moment is now
It has no end and no
Beginning
No top or bottom
No space or distance
Nothing to hold it, mold it, or make
It into anything
It is nothing
And everything
It is all the space in between
It is darkness enveloped
In light

Jessica Dean
Portland, OR

There Are Some Things I Know for Certain

There are some things I know for certain
Like how sunny days are soon clouded by storms
How every dessert will have its last bite
And how goodbyes always roll off the tongue

I may bite my tongue till blood drips down my throat
Sew my lips shut that it pools in my cheeks
But I do not drown
No, the liquid will always purge

How the goodbye leaves my mouth
As water crashes down from a cliff
And when I cough out those last drops
I'm sorry echoes in my hollow throat

I could not save you from goodbye
Dear Friend, why do you follow that path?
While I lay choking on my words
I draw breath while you dance with mortality

There are some things I know for certain
Like one day I'll follow your path
And even if it leads to a void

I know I will find you again.

Julia Madeleine Froehlich
South Windsor, CT

Parched

I hear the distant thunder
The smell of steam fills my nostrils
Lightning streaks across the sky
Birds fly away from the approaching clouds
A plane heads into the front
Disappearing without a trace
The sky it grows dark
The air it grows still
I hear the pitter patter on my roof
I see the raindrops fall into a puddle
I hear the white noise of the pouring shower
Feel the dampness encroach
Life returned to the dryness
Green the color of healing and health
Flowers start to bud
Grass it grows taller
Walls washed clean of dust
Surfaces rinsed clean
A piece of garbage floats down the gutter
Spinning in the drain
The rain it has come and gone
For now the drought is over
A fleeting reminder
Seeing the power of the rain...

Patrick Joseph Whelan
Holiday, FL

Home Again

HE picked him,
From a litter of eight or nine,
They were all fine specimens of bullmastiff, but he chose The One,
It was a sign as he signed on the bottom line,
When his sire – not its father– passed by nudging his elbow,
His father, a brindle too, but oh so much bigger!
He, the man, managed to scribble his name on the contract,
Sealing the deal when the Big One seems to speak saying,
"Take care of my son, you are his father now."
Then approached the next adopter who also froze in awe and respect.
Did the man just become a dog or did the puppy become a human being?
Maybe several measures of both,
For the personable puppy proved to be smart and had the most admirable
human traits,
And brought out the innocent child in the man,
And the man grew to truly love the canine – his constant shadow - as one
of his own.
With the passing of time, they became the proverbial and inseparable boy
and his dog.
While time continued the chase, the man became older,
But his once small bundle of frisky puppy was now old and dying.
When Zeke died, he was mourned with the bountiful sorrows of bitter
loss,
Having made his family and all who knew him better human beings,
We lost indifference between species (and a dear companion) but were
taught a greater humanity, by a dog named Zeke.

George Edward Pope
Brandywine, MD

God's Gift to Man

He loved me!
For God gave His only son
Reflections of the heavens and sun
Perennials
Sophisticated hearts and minds
How much more to adore
The love of all men
Shining upon me
Abundant Life
For it is by grace you have been saved
We all can find a virtuous woman
Believe upon His name
May not come when you want Him
And my message from God is *on time*
This do in remembrance of me
The beast described in biblical text
Whores of Babylon
God's tunnel vision
Today's and tomorrow's daily devotional
In Your name I pray
Amen

Shanette Kay Forte
Texarkana, TX

I Dream of a World Where Color and Hatred Will Not Exist

I dream a world where color will be no more.
I dream a world where hatred and anger will turn to love and peace.
I dream a world of unity of we all need each other in our, own special way.
If I could change the world from this hostility and pain.
I would start from the children to the adults.
I would sing songs of beauty and happiness.
I would let them know that they are blessed and loved.
I will give them all kinds of things to build there confidence in oneself.
I would be an example through my expression and stand of encouragement.
I would let them know that life is worth living.
At, the end of the day.
It doesn't matter who you pray too.
Just know that we all can be of one foundation.
No more fear or destruction.
No more heavy burdens.
I dream a world, where kids are laughing and playing with each other.
Facial expressions of let's have fun.
Until, Mommy and Daddy comes.
Ask, Yourself what color is love and does it exist in your world of good and plentiful.

Fontina Duhart
Delanco, NJ

Joy of Forgiveness

I ask you to think for a moment
ponder if you will the joy of forgiveness.
does it not warm your spirit?
Your emotions have flown from your soul.
now you can stand tall,feel renewed.
you see, there is hope on the horizon
knowing God has forgiven brings peace.
and one can partake of his love.
yet, how did you feel
when you were the forgiver.
Should the feelings of forgiveness
and being forgiven be the same.
yes, yes but why.
is it not from our Heavenly Father?
who asks us to forgive as he forgives.
it is with his pure love for us.
and as we forgive as Christ has
 then it is the same
now we are free from carrying a heavy burden
enjoy the new found peace.
we have partaken of the atonement
there in lays the Joy of Forgivness.

Melvin Gene Perkins
Paris, ID

Invisibly Obvious

I cry
But no one ever sees my tears
This pain
Has been haunting me for years
Afraid
The anxiety is despicable
Self hate
To the naked eye remains invisible
I pray
Asking whomever for some guidance
My mind
Falls momentarily into blissful silence
I sigh
As the sadness suddenly renews the fears
I cry
But no one ever sees my tears

Chantel Scartozzi
Midvale, UT

Decomposition in Four Acts

Before, i had only ever seen dead things in
photographs, but you described to me in detail
what a corpse looks like after months in the ground
and i walked around for the rest of the day
    finding bodies in mirrors

The basement has been
flooded for so many weeks there is
mold growing in every
    west-facing room

Buried the cat in the backyard a decade ago.
How foolish, to hope that the rain would dredge up
    anything other than bones

After all, you can't unhaunt
    a haunted house

Hana Holmgren
Kalamazoo, MI

The Box

I have a box with all these things,
broken glass and angel's wings,
a jar of tears you didn't know you cried,
it's alright.
You be the dreamer and I'll make a wish.
You've been the prisoner and I've been
the victim but together we'll run.
You watch for demons and I'll watch for
monsters.
We will wear garments of white.
You be the hero and I'll be the songbird
that never got to take flight.
Lets make believe there's light at the
end of the tunnel.
Let's pretend we will ever fit in.
You put your secrets in my box for safe
keeping and maybe we'll start again.

Desiree Renee Rodriguez
Platteville, CO

Our Once Upon a Time

All the shades are drawn now,
Candle was getting low.
Moon and stars are hiding,
Candles losing their glow.

All dusty fingerprints!
Someone wiped them clean.
Off from every surface,
They never will be seen.

Mail box is empty,
That once owned someone's name.
Intuition tells me
Nothing will be the same!

The house key it's worthless,
And camouflaged with rust.
Never need to use it,
Once doors opened with trust!

Seems it's all for nothing,
Our once upon a time.
What is still remaining?
The essence you were kind.

Alice Janowski
Hanover Township, PA

The Night

The night she died was the worst,
She was my friends first.
Now she's dead,
Laying her head on her coffin bed
The night, the night she died.

Ember Gibson
Borden, IN

Me

All my life, I wanted what you had.
It all seemed so simple, so happy.
But you chose to hurt us instead.
You chose to hurt me.
Three years later, no difference.
I notice the little things, the little things is what hurts me.
Switching rooms, arguments, the papers.
You both raised me, why can't you see?
You may think you're doing the right thing,
but you're breaking me.
I hate to choose, hate to be put in this situation.
It's okay, because I choose me.

Destiny Farris
Godfrey, IL

To My Precious Ones

I want to draw a picture with colorful butterflies
With magnificent waterfalls and rare birds in the sky
I want to write a story, the most lovely one,
To come straight from the bottom of my heart

I want to build an incredibly beautiful bridge
To connect this world with the world of your dreams
I want to plant spring flower seeds
To see them grow into the tallest tree.

I want to paint a rainbow in the sky
And with a magic stick turn it into a playful slide
I want to breathe in everything you don't need
And breathe out everything You are dreaming about

I want to create for you the most beautiful world
Because since you came into my life
You are my entire world!!!

Evangelia Joseph
Bronx, NY

Fake News

You won't surly die. From beginning Satan has told this lie
Drugs won't destroy, assault rifles won't kill, none of it is real
Take your drugs Satan says; guns won't kill masses like you read
Opioids prescribed for aches and pain; FDA approved it's true
Heroin cocaine it's safe, too; none of this will kill or destroy you
Who says statistic is true; drugs and guns will kill you
It's all fake news

Many of your friends tried . . . drugs, guns . . . many of them died
Don't believe the snake oil media sells—Satan lies
Opioids killed my sister, brother, too; mother cried . . . so will you
Don't believe Satan; nothing he says is true
Drugs demand you do what you vowed not to do
Steal from grandma, your mom who birthed, nursed you
Comfort you, washed, cooked, cleaned and prayed for you
No fake news

Satan is real; he steals your dignity, your days, your years
Don't be fooled my friend, be bold; he wants your soul
He hates you, your friends, your family, your god too
I'm speaking you the truth; Satan kills, not the mentally ill
Run fast friend. Kick Satan in his eye; he won't surely die
I'm speaking you truth; God is love—that's no fake news

Emily M. Mathis
Fort Worth, TX

Dream

When, in the night you wake,
Emptiness surrounds your mind.
When, in the night you wake,
Silence fills your soul.
When, I'm the night you wake,
Darkness blinds your eyes.
Eyes of loss,
Eyes of sorrow,
Eyes of solitude.
When, in the night you wake,
Wrap your mind in soothing rest.
When, in the night you wake,
Still your soul in placid bliss.
When, in the night you wake,
Let dreams caress you from within.

Eldon Raudebaugh
Nashville, TN

Happy Birthday, Daddy

Happy Birthday, Daddy
I can't believe you are 70 now!
You have surprised us all
By making it somehow!
Looking back over the years
You worked as hard as you played
And I am sure you believed
It would be worth it someday.
I hate to inform you,
But "someday" is gone.
It passed right by you
As you pressed on.
Year after year
Day after day
Always providing for your family
In every possible way.
You truly are a warrior
Stronger than you let us see
And I appreciate all you do
Dad, you mean the world to me!

Erika Anya McCarver
Galt, CA

Some Thoughts on Life...

It's about dreaming.
It's about being. More than you thought you could be.
It's about knowing that you matter.

It's about starting.
It's about choosing. To do your best.
It's about loving. Yourself and others.

It's about practice.
It's about showing up.
It's about doing a little extra.

It's about celebrating.
It's about having that cupcake.
It's about dancing in your chair.

It's about focusing.
It's about trying and then tweaking.
It's about smiling when you go to bed at night.

It's about inspiring. Yourself and others.
It's about leaving the world better than you found it.
It's about living. And dying. With no regrets.

Jessica L. Williams
Chicago, IL

Time

As i am here time goes by.
Like the season and the weather that's changing.
The flowers and tree and in a quiet breeze.
As you walk or run the time does not stop.
The day of the light and darkness that come's.
Time will always be for all you can not escape.
I thank you all for the time you take.
Enjoy yourself before it to late.
Coming and going in and out.
Happy and sad day by day.
For time will not wait.
Love and hate do not be late.
Laughing and crying for your sake.
Time is time and that is all.
Life or death that can not change.
Time does not stop forward it will go.
Love is all we have cost no money.
As time move on so do we.

James W. Mounce
Hohenwald, TN

Early Morning Light

In the early morning light,
As you lay sleeping by my side
I awake and gaze at you,
And my heart swells up with pride.
I brush my fingers down your cheek,
And feel the velvet of your skin
I place a kiss upon your brow,
Then another on your chin.
In the early morning light,
A soothing peace drifts in the air
I move my body close to yours,
To breathe the perfume of your hair.
I think of all the years gone by,
And the joy you've brought to me
And the tears that fill my eyes,
Spring from blissful memories.
In the early morning light,
As the world starts turning bright.
I love to hold you in my sight,
In the early morning light.

J. E. Deegan
Spring, TX

Together Apart

From my white winter wonderland
To your beautiful beaches of sand
It doesn't matter what separates you from me
From the cold of Minnesota blistering
To the warmth of Hawaii breeze whispering
Together in love we'll always be
No matter the distance
Or time taken to travel
Your heart's beautiful existence
Causes all barriers to unravel
You are here in my heart
You are always on my mind
Even though we're apart
Our souls are intertwined

Jamison Zrust
Kapolei, HI

The Work Day Is Over

It was one Thursday evening when a man by the name of Tyras decided to be the hero of the day.

When he woke up Thursday morning, he didn't know it was going to be his last morning that he would wake up;

his fiancé didn't know it was going to be the last morning they would share together and most of all;

his son didn't know it was going to be the last day he was going to be able to go to work with his "dada".

As the day went on, Tyras heard the call that he needed to put on his super hero suit even though it meant he had to risk his life.

Tyras picked up his son to protect him as the villain approached.

He instantly went into hero mode because he loved his son just that much and at about 5:11 pm Tyras's heroic task was put to the test.

While Tyras was holding his son, he was stung by bravery and a few moments later, he was stung by courage all to protect his one and only son.

After Tyras was stung by bravery and courage, he heard the call from God saying, "The work day is over."

Thank you, Tyras! Job well done! You've done what you had to do as a hero; now your work on Earth is complete.

Your work and your legacy will forever live on!

Jylan Ross
Lexington, KY

Dig Deep

Dig way deep
And you will find,
The happiness you had
You will still find.

It's in the memories
We all do share,
You don't have to go far
As they are still there.

Just look ahead
But don't look back,
Storms don't last forever
And that is a fact.

Climb up and beyond
Just do your best,
You got to believe
Let the Lord do the rest.

Judith Rae Andrews
Indianapolis, IN

Desert Street Person

He's tall and too thin,
standing in the middle
of the street, shouting
to someone or something
invisible at the top of a palm.

I stop my car while he rants
in front of me and finally
steps back onto the sidewalk.
By the time I park my car,
he's there, still reciting
whatever it is he says.

Maybe it's a prayer
he prayed as a child.
Maybe it's a mandate
from his mother
to stay off drugs.
"It will fry your brain,"
she kept telling him.

But he didn't listen,
and took drugs anyway
to forget the mistakes
he made growing up,
or to remember not
to make the same ones twice.

Jauren Miller
Palm Springs, CA

Mechanical Bull

As the mechanical bull picked up speed
The rider pressed in harder with both his knees
Five seconds had gone by, he was on the floor
This old cowboy won't be riding anymore.

He had too much to drink, but he had to ride
An old bronc-busting cowboy with too much pride
His hair was gray, his frame was thin
He wanted to prove to himself that he could ride again

An old cowboy, born on the range
A mechanical bull he thought he could tame
He rode that bull like never before
Then off he went, he was thrown to the floor.

But he needed to ride this one last time
His memory failing from his delirious mind
The old man's smile seemed somewhat strange
Then I knew he was riding on an endless range.

Joseph Sotir Jr.
Abilene, TX

The Tides of Time—Morning's Mercy

The tides of time have finally come and gone
Silently slipping sideways while we looked on
Now the survivors of your Parkinson's
The strange clothes you had to wear at the end
Have all been donated
Your needle point pillow went home with him
Your jewelry will come to me and them in time and turn
To my children
The strengths that coursed through your DNA are locked and loaded
Into mine my son has Viking bones and muscles
My daughter ...my child has as mighty will and takes no prisoners
I am fair of eye and hair as you were
But fairly fading in my due
The grass which I often pondered from the other side of the fence
During the long long walk home with you is indeed wildly sweet and so
So green
I suddenly smell the earth
I taste the earth
I am on the earth far more for your having left it
You sail the sky seas now
I saw you go in a dream and awakened to morning's mercy

Ingrid Showalter Swift
Dennis, MA

A Second Chance

We search to find
That love devine
So once when found
We do abound
Although the time we share remains unclear
We begin our lives without any fear
When one is called because it's time
The need to live again feels like a crime
If love appears as it sometimes may
Open your heart and soul and don't dismay
To feel needed again makes our love worth giving
Sharing your time with another makes life worth living

Jay Block
Rome, NY

I Dream

I dream a dream of happiness.
I dream of a day when sorrow and strife will no longer be a part of my life.
The dream I have is happy and true.
I dream of the day when tears will no longer darken my life.
My life's breath will be free from sorrow and strife.
I dream of a day when I will no longer feel the need to cry out my feelings.
I dream of the day when I will be someone's wife.
But most of all I dream of the day when my parents will love again.

April Katko
New Brunswick, NJ

Beaches

My last thought stuck like mist
To the blue child etching passages
In long forgotten beaches
Where the wind erases history
And verbs are careless scratches
Laced through shells and dying fishes.

If I could claim the language of the wave
Stolen like a woman on a half moon's whim,
Whose white breath blew though me,
Then I could sleep with wild kittens
And satisfy the old dirt's greed.

But I have lost the child,
The maniac scrawling from a bent smile,
And experience claims her victim
On a slash of wasted ink clinging
Thinly to the memory of paper sand.

Catherine K. Hurd
Centerville, TN

A Sad Prayer

Our politicians, who art in Congress.
Halloween be thy name.
Thy committee won,
thy bills get done.
In House as it is in Senate.
Give us this day our raise in tax,
and increase our debt,
as we struggle beneath it.
Lead us not into exemption,
but deliver us from income.
For thine is the earmark,
and the pork barrel,
and the paid for vote forever.
Amen.

Philip Hukill
Hillsdale, MI

The Watchers

They're outside of my window
A passing glance in the street
In the corner of my eye and in my dreams when I'm asleep
Lurking in the shadows shaking me to my core
Waiting in the hallways inside my bedroom door
The Watchers they are called I can't escape their dread .
The Watchers are my grandparents and my grandparents are dead.

China Boynton
Pompano Beach, FL

Strong

As the sun goes down and the moon takes its place
I sit here tonight with tears streaming down my face
My whole life has been chaos and full of broken dreams
I don't think I'll ever be okay, or that is how it seems
My child, My child listen to me
I gave you the toughest battles just so you'd see
The fire inside you burns so bright
Through all the storms you never kept your light
The winds blew as the belts hit your skin
But you kept on fighting, couldn't let him win
I know you didn't understand, but there's a reason for it all
What really matters is what you do after the fall
There's a reason you were given this life
You had to find your strength before you could be his wife
He needs someone strong enough to face the fire
Someone brave enough to call the devil a liar
He needs your gentleness because he's rough around the edges
He needs your love to hold onto so he can burn his bridges
He needs your courage to fill his heart
And this my child is why I made you strong from the start

Sharon Humphreys
Knoxville, TN

Back to Basics

Fight for freedom; a never-ending fight.
Fight for justice; and what's right.
Fight for our country and our state.
With God on our side; it's not too late.
Hearts joined together in one accord.
We must keep it clean; spread the word.
We don't need hate and ugly disputes.
We don't need all these uncalled for refutes.
We need honesty and upright virtues.
Not lies and nasty untruths.
Getting back to basics as God intended.
To love, be friends, hearts be mended.
Put God and His Word back in our lives.
We want good for our world. We want to survive.

Carolyn J. Fisher
Winter Park, FL

Under the Misletoe

Under the mistletoe is where I want to meet with you.
A simple exchange and a kiss for love and luck, just as tradition tells us to.
If this is our place of meeting, let's plant mistletoe all around the world
times two.
A chance to spend precious time with my love and my very best
friend—the one whom I have found in you.
Merry Christmas 2019
Under the Misletoe

Rahsaan Faraji Foster
Bonner Springs, KS

Cherry Pit

Time continues flowing
But very little changes
   Besides location; there have
  Been no provocations nor
  Much rain for even grains

   Life without emotional pain
   Would be better if there was
  Somewhere to go every day
     And someone with whom to share it
  Preferably without having a fit

   Except for being happy this day
   Or even once and awhile how can
   I not sometimes feel as if a cherry
  Pit that has fallen into grits?

John Long
Grayland, WA

More Than Words

Silence
But there is sound.
Movement
But all is still.
Sun
But it remains dark.
Wind
But no breeze can be felt.
Crying
But there are no tears falling.
Yelling
But there are no voices.
Rain
But the ground remains dry.
Night
But it is daylight.
Chirping
But there are no birds.
Smell
But no odor.

Jennifer Cherry
Muldrow, OK

Not with You

When you are not with me
I feel this empty space
Close to my heart
When you are with me
I feel like there nothing
That can go wrong
When you are not with me
I miss your touch
When you hold my hand
The way you kiss me
How sweet you lips taste
The way you look at me
With those eyes of yours
I want to be with you
Forever and eternity

Andy Guidry
Colorado Springs, CO

Dead

Wicked in flesh
Devil possessed scripture
Unmasked evil encrypted
Unasked questions and vengeance
Symptoms
Infects insect
Sickness and death
Echoes each breath
Leeches eat at my neck
Loch ness creature left its nest
In a mess more or less
As a last request
Unimpressed
Wishing for the best
Depressed wish heart would quit
Just quit and not restart again
Then skin could begin rotting
Body embalming
Haunted and falling
Darkness is calling
Darling you coming
The monster's been summoned
The ending is dawning
Just end it by morning
Been dead since 20

Zachary Tayler Reed
Gainesville, TX

Consuming

Exercising self-control
When hints itch
In empty moments.
Shared fulfilling exchange
With yet another ghost—
Difficult conversations
Are honest ones.
Attempting to name
One instance where
Phantom thought
Has changed her
For the better.
Got too high
The night prior,
Waking up to
Swollen cheeks and
Jagged flesh
Can be tender.
Introducing importance
As a poltergeist:
Shifted, lifted, misplaced.
She is intoxication
In the same way
She is daybreak—
Consuming

—But what do they care?

Carly Ransdell
Brooklyn, NY

A Caregiver's Point of View

People often ask what makes care giving worthwhile
To me it's the respect and their smile
As I have always had a giving heart
I've always tried to help and do my part
There were days I'd struggle and was grim
Everything seemed to change the day I met him
The day my journey lead me to a wonderful gentleman
That was the day my professional relationship truly began
Before meeting you, I felt I hadn't given enough
After meeting you, you taught me to be tough
When my heart had lost all hope
You gave the courage to cope
You seemed to go that long and extra mile
Just to see my heart laugh and smile
Then came the day you took your final sigh
You had to leave without saying goodbye
Even though your days here are through
My memories of you keep me from being blue
You and I will never be far apart
Because you taught me
"I've got a golden heart"

Kimberly Hildenbrand
Oconto, WI

Thinking of You

As I sit here I can only think of you,
    and I wonder with whom.
I think of all the fun we had.
I think of how your smile could make me glad.
How your frown could make me sad.

I think of the birds singing from the trees.
I think of the skies high above.
I wonder if you know how much I care.
How much I think of you.

I think of you and me alone together.
The way it should always be.
I think of how sad it made me.
When you wanted to be free.

I think of how you called me a dreamer.
This I know is true.
I think if you ask yourself a question,
Am I a dreamer too?

I think of how you told me to grow up.
This I have done.
I think of how you told me there is someone else.
I must tell you, you are my only one.

I think of how we are apart.
I want us together again.
If this moment cannot happen.
I want us to be friends.

I think of how I must tell you.
A few words left unsaid.
In my heart,
    I am still in love with you.

Ann Marie Trimm
Romoland, CA

Sweet Beach That Raised Me

Sand that hugs my feet,
Please embrace me.
Raise me like the tidal waves,
And drag me back when you have uneasy feelings.
Water that sets me a drift,
Protect me from the monsters who swim beneath us.
Don't pull me under with your vicious tsunami when thy waves are
tampered.
Because I'll be there to calm your soul.
Sun that sets on the horizon,
You're so beautiful.
Light the path for me to follow after you have risen me.
Thank you for your natural nurture.
You've lead me to my own destiny.
Goddess, Body of water,
sweet beach that raised me,
Let me leave this beach and make my own stream.
Let it drip into its own ocean.
So my sand can hug her feet.
So I can raise her like the tidal waves,
And bring her back when I have uneasy feelings.
For I am my own body of water now.
But please don't feel tampered with
I am still here to calm your soul
And comfort you.

Ashley Woody
Conyers, GA

Another Statistic

Another life gone, another friend lost.
The cravings get too high, no matter the cost.
Kids lose their parents and families are torn apart.
The battle in your mind rages, begging you not to start.
The war in your brain like a battle, because you know what's right from
wrong.
But often we know from experience, the urges are just too strong.
We forget about the other people in our lives; we focus just on ourselves.
Not wanting to feel life's pains, we think about nothing else.
Addiction, baffling and powerful, will tell us getting high is fun.
But the statistics are stacked against us; will this be the last one?
Time is running short; it's like playing Russian roulette.
Knocking on death's door, you soon will pay its debt.
So will you make the choice and fight to NOT get high.
Or will you become another statistic—another friend who's died?

Christine Arboe
Willimantic, CT

Lost & Found

Followed some voices to a revival tent
but I soon got confused on what they really meant
So I summoned some spirit, but soon asked it to go
It was bringing me down, saying there's no more answers to these
questions we know
Ran into a cult, that was fun for a day
But they're smiles soon made me nervous when they insisted that I stay
So I walked until I came upon a mosque all gaudy with gold
The local Rabbi had donated, or so I was told
My head started swimming so I ventured deep into the wood
Brought me closer to something bigger than me than any religion ever
could
So the next time you're bothered by some bloody holy war
Try not to shed too many tears, there's been a few before
and a few more in store
Oh! What a shame!
Lost ones finding the found ones
going astray every single second of every day
Oh! Who's to blame?
But do you really think my life would be any different today?
Lost ones can be found around the bend
Evil nature separates us in the end
Look around you and don't dare pretend
that you might need to know everything that will be, my friend.

Scott Wolfhope
Greenbrier, TN

The Pull of the Tide

You tell me I am the moon,
ever present and beautiful,
always finding a way to shine
regardless of the darkness that surrounds everything,
stretching out as far as the eye can see
and going on for all of eternity.
You tell me I am the moon
because I have been there for you day after day,
night after night, through thick and thin.
I'm the one who saw you through your fight.
You tell me I am the moon,
stardust dancing across my cheeks,
silver streaming across the sky as my heart weeps.
You tell me that even if I feel alone
I have thousands of stars to keep me company,
they're all right there in front of me, yet I can't see
because none of them can compare to my light.
And you expect me to believe you, right?
Yes, there's beauty in the moon
but who can love the moon once you've known the sun?
If I'm the moon, my light is the reflection of other's,
just another cover, another mask to say I'm okay.
If I'm the moon then darkness is always surrounding me,
but the sun, the light is something I never see.
I'm just alone, held in place by some unknown force
but drifting away all the same.

Anna Bryant
Stockton, MO

He Knew

GOD knew what he was doing
When he placed inside you a seed;
Think about the less fortunate,
Who will never be able to concieve.

Theirs no value that can
Replace the joy they bring;
You were given the best gifts of all,
Giving life to those precious human beings.

For all the times you sacrificed
Just to buy them new shoes; or
The times you worked overtime
So they could have some food.

You are being celebrated for all
That you do,
From Mother to Mother, we all
Think you're really cool.

Hang in there your time
Will surely come,
Know your truly blessed and
Your acts of love can't be outdone!

Carlise L Ballard
Jacksonville, FL

Rsd

I know that you said "I can't play,
Tomorrow, 'haps, but not today,"
Yet all I hear is "Go away."

To fight the fire of demon's tongue
Stone-cold reason won't suffice
Impassioned chimes of emotion rung
Shatter logic with a lash of ice

They mean no harm, my friends and peers
But still my mind, its wretched gears
Whirling madly, concocting fears,
An unloved life, this feeling's brung

Perhaps it was a quick remark,
A careless jab, unmeaning stab
Caught unawares, shot in the dark
Thus I retreat elsewhere to scab

O dreaded thoughts, unfair, untrue!
Unhand my brain, I beg of you!
'Else think of something new to do
than tease my nightmares, mindset skew...

For once, I'm glad my focus isn't
quite on-point, as I'm told it ought
Least then, dysphoric chantings shan't
stick to me long, attention fraught
Toward frenzies new and memories not
Organized thoughts, I haven't got

'Fraid I've quite forgotten, now,
from where exactly my distress arose
Oh well. It'll be back, somehow,
when I least expect it, I suppose
In matters of mind, anything goes.

AJ Smith
Mead, WA

We Serve

We serve...we fight.
Are we doing it right?
We serve...we fight.
To protect human life.
We serve ...we fight.
Is it a human right?
We serve...we fight.
Where's God? Who's in charge?
Is he/she out of sight or in the background "trying to do it right"
Who to call when we fall?
Are we wrong?
Why can't we get along?
All blood is "red"...how many of us fell dead?
How is our love going to spread?
Is there still time to change this world back to the divine?
Or are we all going to hell when the Divine cast His heavenly spell?

Rev. Olivia L. Armstrong
Columbia, SC

Terra Mater

I'm choking
It's so hard to breathe
The air is so thick and heavy
Inside of me it sits then swirls

I can't see
My eyes are blocked by heavy gray clouds
They span in every direction
They cover me

I'm thirsty
The water inside is dirty
There's nothing clean left
Every drink is full of chemicals

I'm hungry
The food I have is scarce
What's inside is rotted
I'm starving down to the bone

I'm dying
People have beat me up and thrown me away
So few have cared
Nobody sees it

Help me

Alexander Eugene Hicks
Pensacola, FL

INDEX OF POETS

A

Adkins, Chris 183
Albis, Kirsten Louise 65
Aldridge, Sue 209
Alexandre, Jordan Rex 186
Amaro, Nic 87
Andrews, Judith Rae 243
Arboe, Christine 260
Armstrong, Olivia L. 265

B

Babbit, D. M. 127
Backalenick, Irene 1
Baker, Tess 36
Bakhos, Friday 156
Ballard, Carlise L. 263
Ballard, Liza Marie 201
Barnes, Richard A. 152
Bauer, Ted J. 192
Bavington, Bette Anne 14
Beason, Kristy D. 62
Beco, Quiana Nikita 206
Belanger, Theresa Ann 15
Bellamy, Jeffrey 171
Bennet, Sirigrid 149
Bergman, Lawrence 75
Bettis, Macayla 134
Billingsley, Aria J. 129
Blackmon, Zoe Angela 181
Block, Jay 247
Bong, Kyle 54
Bowers, Tiana M. 31
Boynton, China 249
Brantley, Jodie 78
Breese, Richard 25
Brown, Derhone 181
Brown, Reginald 18

Brummett, Charlotte Diana 192
Bryant, Anna 262
Buonocore, Matt 108
Burciaga, Melissa L. 193
Butts, Piper Elisabeth 17

C

Cain, Lori I. 99
Calabrese, Linda Lee 52
Cammarata, Esme 165
Campbell, Elizabeth J. 91
Camp, Marissa Leigh 103
Cannon, Amber 169
Carlock Clark, Morgan 106
Carter, Patricia Jean 184
Carter, Tammy L. 204
Cedres, Sandra Ivette 134
Chaffin, Hannah Lily 202
Chambers, Morgen Mariah 90
Cherry, Jennifer 253
Chesley, Thomas 143
Chocron, Sarah Flora 10
Clavo, Maria 88
Cline, Irene J. 218
Comer, Jessica 200
Cooke, Ryan 151
Cooksey, Patty D. 142
Craig, Michael 213
Craig, Michael Lee 123
Cwalina, Kira Anne 66

D

DaBolt, Trisha 37
Darlow, Shelly J. 28
Daugherty, Susan C. 58
Davila-Aponte, Mary Beth 184

Davis, Jaelynn 221
Dawley, Carol Sue 161
Dean, Jessica 222
Deegan, J. E. 240
Delacruz, Maria Fernanda 195
Deloch, Kierra Nicole 67
DeWitt, Samantha 58
Diaz, Dianna 4
Diggs, Jianna Joy 137
Dillard, Amber J. 144
Duhart, Fontina 227
Dunlap, Scot 119
Dunning, Krystal 64
Dunn, Kristin 168
Dutkin, Joan 122

E

Elizabeth, Katharine 217
Elkins, Kristan E. 61
Ellis, Albert Ashton 128
Enos, Gary Wayne 175
Evans, Anai 77
Evans, Tiffany 30

F

Farris, Destiny 233
Fisher, Carolyn J. 251
Flowers, Shirley J. 51
Forte, Shanette Kay 226
Foster, Rahsaan Faraji 251
Fournier, Stephen 54
Franklin, Faith Gabbrielle 146
Frankston, Jay 40
Froehlich, Julia Madeleine 223
Frontiero, Corinne 167
Fulcomer, James Michael 81

G

Gahm, Amanda D. 9
Gaide, Marsha 212
Gammon, Valerie Ann 45

Garcia, Renee Edna 138
Garza, Alejandro Noel 33
Gates, Teresa O. 30
Gibson, Ember 233
Gibson, Lavette 73
Godfrey, Sherry 42
Goins, Precious Ikia 13
Goodman, Mackenzie 78
Grove, Heather Dawn 211
Guidry, Andy 254

H

Hall, Jack 107
Hare, Michael 105
Harkey Bratton, Robin 199
Harmon, Troy Michael 162
Hebert, Haley 155
Hedin, Jessica Jo 138
Henderson, Chloe 164
Henderson, Lisa Loraine 110
Hicks, Alexander Eugene 266
Hildenbrand, Kimberly 257
Hollander, Mary Ann 114
Holley, Shelby John 3
Holmgren, Hana 230
Holt, Mary E. 111
Hope, Margaret 200
Horton, Tamara L. 135
Howard, Antwanette L. 123
Hukill, Philip 249
Humphreys, Sharon 250
Hunter, Elizabeth 166
Hunter, Jessica 219
Hurd, Catherine K. 248

J

Jackson, Kataya Chelise 194
Jackson, Paige Elizabeth 97
Janowski, Alice 232
Jean-Baptiste, Nagella 109
Johnson, Don 84
Johnson, Natashia 84
Jones, Kaitlyn Elizabeth 118

Jones, Madison 142
Jones, Sarah Elizabeth 12
Joseph, Evangelia 234
Juarez, Maria 182

K

Kalaparampath, Elsy Paulose 159
Katko, April 247
Katkus, Mea 187
Kaufman, Susan 59
Kerchner, Rena E. 21
Khoshnobish, Sumaya 68
Kinerk, Robert R. 218
Klareich, Lee 72
Kohles, John Keith 80
Kornutiak, Steve 141
Krzewinski, Kathy Renee 20
Kubie, Christian Charles 50

L

Langston, Maryah 112
Larson, Travis Anthony 29
Laughlin, Korynn 215
Leake, Alan 188
Lee, Yeeun 213
Lertpradist, Tanya 220
Lewis, Stephanie Marie 48
Long, John 252
Lovalvo, Kimberly 104
Lovekill, Blossom 62
Lundberg, Auna J. 174

M

Magee, Shemar Jaheim 19
Mahoney, Karin 89
Mallahan, John V. 101
Mallgren, Anthony Brian 70
Maloney, Sharon Ann 16
Manivanh, Nia Ariana 98
Manning, Jill Rene 80
Mann, Timmi Jimette 125

Marcus, Kate 154
Martinez Alejandro, Xiomara 39
Mason, Carmie 121
Mason, Moriah Ayana 93
Mathis, Emily M. 235
Matthews, Derick Mitchell 180
Mazique, Nae Chanel 178
McCarver, Erika Anya 237
McIntyre, Ebony J. 153
McKinney, Mary Peyton 208
Mecavica, Lejla 37
Merriman, Amanda 47
Mica, Robert 158
Miller, Jauren 244
Miske, Delilah Ray 193
Mitchell, Revae 13
Mohan, Sharon 133
Morgan, Pallas-Amenah 96
Mounce, James W. 239
M., Rachel Ellynn 27
Murray, Raymond 108

N

Nacke, Robert Louis 120
Nagy-Rizzuto, Sophia Clara 190
Naloev, Malik 177
Nath, Cora Ruth 207
Nelson, Keonna 164
Neubecker, Sarah Catherine 157
Nguyen, Nick James 34
Norfleet, Shanell 7

O

Ohde, Grace E. 147
Okafor, Veronica Nneoma 46
Onokoko, Victoire 44
Orstrom, Israel 173

P

Pal, Sunayna 56
Parsons, Rebecca 32

Patenaude, Marc Adrien 212
Patino, Camilo 95
Paz, Samantha Victoria 197
Pentland, Kathryn Elizabeth 15
Perkins, Melvin Gene 228
Phillip, Angie M. 165
Phinazee, Edith Andrews 139
Photte, Oyéb 100
Pierce, La'niece Brittani 198
Pittman, Nichole 170
Plains, Shanja Marie 6
Platz, Thomas Edward 25
Pope, George Edward 225
Prater, Elizabeth Mae 172
Prince, Madicen Grace 102
Pyles, William Joe 41

R

Raccuglia, Kristie Anne 60
Ransdell, Carly 256
Rasheed, Poet 116
Raudebaugh, Eldon 236
Reed, Zachary Tayler 255
Remyn, Kim 210
Ricks, Christopher 131
Ridenour, Miranda 185
Rightnour, Rebecca Jennalynn 211
Riles, Amanda Josephine 189
Roberts, Madelyn 201
Rocke, Kai 83
Rodriguez, Desiree Renee 231
Rodriguez, Guadalupe B. 2
Rose, Jeremiah Patrick 116
Rosinsky, Kim 24
Ross, Jylan 242
Rounds, Lena Rose 71
Ruch, Jen A. 179
Russell, Teresa 162
Russo, Sophia Joy 49

S

Salim, Sidqieh Nowal 175
Say, Sheilah 205

Scartozzi, Chantel 229
Schnell, Mark Daniel 113
Seang, Sethea 8
Serey, Jody 76
Seuss, Nellie Marie 163
Shaheen, Peter L. 23
Showalter Swift, Ingrid 246
Singh, Sophia 42
Skidmore, Jeremy 115
Small, Daniel S. 110
Smith, AJ 264
Smith, Nya Janelle 216
Smuckler, Allen 196
Snow, Hannah 144
Sotir, Joseph 245
Spear, Jocelyn 79
Staley, Elsa Paige Yuan Yuan 124
Stalnaker, Sonja 32
Stevens, Ashley 109
Stevens, Jessica 55
Stewart, Randi Lynn 26
Stone, Cherry Marie 214
Stoy, Nancy 86
Strauch, Matt 67
Strong, Dani 22
Sunflowers, Daisy Sarah Ray 63
Symmes, Lorelai Madison 61

T

Taylor, Iisha 52
Taylor, Sara Alexandra 53
Thakur, Eesha 148
Thomas, Monica H. 82
Thompson, Youlanda Marie 117
Thornton, Amber Louise 136
Thurston, Krystal 182
Thurston, William Morris 126
Tidmore, Nerissa Christina 99
To, Natasa Cuc 85
Toral, Adare 35
Torres, Noel 94
Tov, Lev 132
Traeger, Noah K. 140
Trimm, Ann Marie 258

Turner, Mark 92
Turner, Summerlynn Marie 57

U

Uncles, Jennifer Nicole 133

V

Vaca, Jeffrey Deleon 156
Valenzuela, Victoria Cipriana 43
Velazquez, Ignacio Jesus 130
Villafranco, Raven M. 203
Vuichoud, Gabriela 176

W

Wadley, Kewayne 69
Watson, Dominique L. 160
Weime, Sharon 5
Welch, Corey 89
West, Marty L. 188
Whelan, Patrick Joseph 224
Williams, Brittany 145
Williams, Cody 150
Williams, Jessica L. 238
Wodlinger, Marcie 152
Wolfhope, Scott 261
Woods, Brittany Lakkia 74
Woody, Ashley 259
Wyley, Sarah 11

Y

Yodhhewawhe, Yehuwdiyth 38
Young, Robert Zedekiah 191

Z

Zrust, Jamison 241

CPSIA information can be obtained
at www.ICGtesting.com
Printed in the USA
FSHW010327300621
82754FS

9 781608 806669